DEATH AND THE RIGHT HAND

Robert Hertz

DEATH
&
THE
RIGHT
HAND

Translated by
RODNEY AND CLAUDIA
NEEDHAM

With an Introduction by
E. E. EVANS-PRITCHARD

THE FREE PRESS
GLENCOE, ILLINOIS

These two works were first published in the French language
in *L'Année Sociologique*, 1907, and *Revue Philosophique*, 1909
Presses Universitaires de France, Editeurs, Paris

PRINTED IN GREAT BRITAIN AT
THE UNIVERSITY PRESS
ABERDEEN

TRANSLATORS' NOTE

In translating these essays we have assumed that when Hertz used a particular word he intended to use that word and not another; and that the length and composition of his sentences, like his use of footnotes, represents his deliberate mode of exposition. It would not have been very difficult otherwise to produce versions which in places would have read rather more easily than the translations we offer; but at every point of literal divergence we should have felt obliged to explain to ourselves why Hertz did not make our choice of word when there was a perfectly good French equivalent. Similarly, we have felt bound to assume that Hertz's grouping of facts and comments displays his notions of relevance or logical connexion; that his punctuation is to an interesting degree part of the way he thought, and that the construction of his prose was meant to present his analysis in a particular manner. In sum, we have tried to convey not only Hertz's arguments but his way of thinking, and we have tried to reflect in our translations the qualities of the original texts. We realise that these principles may have resulted at places in a rather literal air, but what matters in a work of sociological analysis is, we think, exactitude rather than elegance. We have endeavoured, naturally, to write clear and readable English; but at every point of decision we have chosen bare literalness rather than a more pleasing rendition which did not accord with these principles.

Certain changes have been made, however, mainly in the notes and the bibliographical references. The footnotes have been renumbered serially in each essay and brought together after the two texts. The references have been abbreviated and the complete titles have been consolidated in separate bibliographies. Since none of Hertz's references was complete by modern standards we have thought it helpful to supply the details which he omitted; and as he also referred to some sources by titles which were inexact, and was occasionally inaccurate in other particulars, a considerable part of the preparation of this volume has consisted in tracing and checking the authorities. We thank Dr. Peter Suzuki, of the University of Leiden, and M. Olivier Herrenschmidt, of the University of Paris, for their help with certain titles which were not discoverable in this country. A few titles nevertheless could not be found and remain incomplete or dubious.

Hertz's page-references have not for the most part been checked, but where they have been they have nearly always proved correct. The case is different with his quotations from the authorities he consulted, for although his versions correctly convey the sense they are commonly paraphrases rather than exact translations. In most instances, therefore, we have not referred to the originals or reproduced the sources of quotations from English but have simply translated Hertz's French.

Proper names in the text have been changed from Dutch, German or French orthography to forms more appropriate to an English edition: e.g. Bejadjoe to Beyaju, Ngadju to Ngaju, Alfourou to Alfuru. Literary titles have not been altered, and neither have references to words in dictionaries: thus the Ngaju word of which the Germanic rendering is *tiwah* is written as *tivah* (which in English orthography is nearer to its pronunciation) except in the title of Grabowsky's essay or when the reader is directed to the entry under that word in Hardeland's dictionary.

We should like to thank Professor Evans-Pritchard, who in his lectures at Oxford University first commended Hertz's work to our admiration, for contributing the Introduction and for his continued interest in the production of these translations.

R. N.
C. N.

Oxford

CONTENTS

7

INTRODUCTION

By E. E. Evans-Pritchard

Professor of Social Anthropology and
Fellow of All Souls College, Oxford

IN the last few years there have been published translations by past and present members of the Institute of Social Anthropology at Oxford of two minor classics of the French sociological school, Emile Durkheim's thesis on the relations between philosophy and sociology and Marcel Mauss's essay on gift-exchange.[1] A third volume is now presented, a translation of two essays by Robert Hertz,[2] a pupil of Durkheim and a friend of Mauss and a little-known, because short-lived, writer. These essays I have greatly admired, and I have lectured on them at Oxford for a number of years. Dr. Needham has shared my admiration and he and Mrs. Needham have gladly devoted much time to translating them. It is appropriate that Dr. Needham should have undertaken this task, because Hertz specialized in Indonesian studies, a field in which he is himself an acknowledged authority. These three translations have been published by the same publishers both in England and in the United States and in the same format, so we hope they may be the beginning of a series of such translations, which are not just translations of unconnected essays but of essays which have a close theoretical relationship, each illustrating in the discussion of a particular topic a common point of view. If it should prove to be possible we will add

---

[1] Emile Durkheim, *Sociology and Philosophy*, translated by D. F. Pocock with an introduction by J. G. Peristiany, 1953; Marcel Mauss, *The Gift*, translated by Ian Cunnison with an introduction by E. E. Evans-Pritchard, 1954.

[2] 'La représentation collective de la mort', and ' La prééminence de la main droite '.

to the series other translations of important essays by writers of the *Année Sociologique* school.

What is the point of publishing these translations? I would answer that if the essays are still worth reading they are worth translating, for there are many people in the world, among them students of sociology and social anthropology, who have English as a mother or second tongue and have no, or a very inadequate, knowledge of the French language; and I believe that they are still worth reading, although written many years ago, for their historical, methodological, and theoretical interest.

Durkheim had gathered around him in Paris between 1902 and 1914 a group of younger students, some of whom were killed in the 1914–18 war, among them Hertz, while others died during or shortly after the war, as did the Master himself, in 1917. The school of the *Année Sociologique* survived these tragic losses, mostly through the courage and industry of Mauss, but it cannot be said that it ever recovered from them.

Robert Hertz was killed leading his section in the attack on Marchéville on 13 April 1915, at the age of thirty-three. He had already published the essays presented here, which represent only a peripheral interest to the study on which he was engaged, of sin and expiation, and he had planned a book on these complementary ideas in primitive societies (*Le Péché et l'Expiation dans les Sociétés inférieures*), the almost completed introduction to which appeared posthumously.[1] He had also published an article, based on a field study, of the cult of Saint Besse;[2] and the folklore notes he took down from his men at the front and sent to his wife were published in 1917.[3] He had also written a socialist brochure.[4] In 1928

---

[1] ' Le Péché et l'Expiation dans les Sociétés primitives ', *Revue de l'Histoire des Religions*, 1922. Mauss says (*Année Sociologique*, Nouvelle Série, Tome I, 1925, p. 24) that he hoped to publish the whole book, but it never appeared. Another work by Hertz, on the myth of Athena, was left in a sufficiently completed state to be published, but it also has not been.

[2] 'Saint Besse', *Revue de l'Histoire des Religions*, 1913.

[3] 'Contes et Dictons', *Revue des Traditions Populaires*, 1917.

[4] *Socialisme et Dépopulation* (Les Cahiers du Socialiste, No. 10), 1910.

Mauss brought together in one volume[1] the essays on death
and the right hand, the article on the cult of Saint Besse,
and a lengthy review by Hertz of a book by K. K. Grass on
an ascetic and ecstatic Russian sect, the Khluists.[2]

Robert Hertz's widow, Alice Hertz (*née* Bauer), who died
while her husband's collected essays were in the press,
tells us in her preface to them of his enthusiasm for his
researches (largely carried out in the British Museum in
1904–06) and how, in a sense, he lived with the Dayaks of
Borneo, even learning their language, so that they became
for him not just figures in his notebooks but flesh and blood.
However, he came to realize that such a study from books
could never equal experience at first-hand when in the long
vacation of 1912 he began his study of the cult of Saint
Besse, that curious figure garbed in the uniform of a Roman
legionary, in the remote Alpine community of Cogne, near
Aoste. 'How much more alive than the work in the library,
this direct contact with realities just as rich in possibilities
as the rites of primitives at the other end of the earth.'

The historical value of Hertz's writings is that they are a
representative example of the culmination of two centuries
of development of sociological thought in France, from
Montesquieu to Durkheim and his pupils. I cannot attempt
to trace even an outline of this development here. It must
suffice to say that a survey of the intervening years shows
how philosophical speculation, often highly didactic and
illustrated with the barest information about the simpler
societies—those with which Durkheim and his school mainly
dealt—has grown into the systematic comparative study of
primitive institutions, based on a great body of ethnographic
facts collected from all over the world, which in the British
Isles we call social anthropology. I regard Fustel de
Coulanges's *La Cité antique* (1864) as the dividing point
between the speculative and dogmatic treatises of such
writers as Turgot, Condorcet, Saint-Simon and Comte on
the one side, and on the other, for example, Durkheim's
detailed analyses of systems of classification, totemism, and

---

[1] Robert Hertz, *Mélanges de Sociologie Religieuse et Folklore*, 1928.
[2] This was written for the *Année Sociologique* but was not printed there.

incest prohibitions, and Hubert and Mauss's scholarly treatment of sacrifice and magic.[1] And the movement towards a truly scientific study of social phenomena was continuing and has continued. In Durkheim's writings facts are still sometimes subordinated to an *a priori* philosophical doctrine. This is much less so in the essays of Hubert and Mauss and in Hertz's writings, though even in them some of the formulas which clouded Durkheim's mind remain, as, for example, the appeal to a collective consciousness, a vague and ill-defined conception, and to the dichotomy of sacred and profane, a polarity which I find to be almost equally vague and ill-defined. There remains also Durkheim's irritating manoeuvre, when a fact contradicts his thesis, of asserting that its character and meaning have altered, that it is a secondary development and atypical, although there is no evidence whatsoever that such changes have taken place.

These essays have also a methodological interest. The method employed was that dignified in England by the name of 'the comparative method', a title which means little more than that if one wishes to make a general statement about the nature of some institution one has first to examine it in a number of different societies. Social philosophers have been making such comparisons through the centuries. What else was Aristotle doing in the *Politics* or Machiavelli in *The Prince*? However, among the anthropologists of the last century and up to the present time it was claimed that a more rigorous use of the comparative method, especially by establishing correlations, would yield scientific formulations which might legitimately be called laws.

The method includes two different operations. In the first, what is done is to separate out the general from the particular and the social fact from its cultural form, thereby making a classification of types or categories of general

---

[1] Though I am not aware that he anywhere says so, I think that Fustel de Coulanges, and also, of course, Montesquieu, had a greater formative influence on Durkheim's thought than Saint-Simon and Comte. Would one be wrong in detecting also the influence of de Tocqueville?

social phenomena. This procedure enabled the anthropologists of the last century to bring to notice that such institutions as marriage by capture, totemism, matrilineal descent, taboo, exogamy, and various systems of kinship nomenclature are widespread and everywhere have the same essential characteristics in spite of a great variety of forms. The data for comparison were thus classified for further study. This is what Hertz did in these essays when he isolated two significant facts with a very wide distribution among the simpler peoples, a second burial, or at any rate mortuary ceremony, and the association of a variety of ideas and values with the right and left hands. In his study of second burials he drew attention to the large number of different forms disposal of a corpse takes in different societies but pointed out that these differences need not be taken into account in making a sociological analysis since the procedures have the same purpose and function.

A class of facts having been isolated for study, the second operation is to reach certain conclusions about them. How this operation is conducted depends on what sort of conclusions are aimed at. Encouraged by the successful use of the comparative method in other disciplines, especially in philology, anthropologists of the last century expected that it would provide them with a means of reconstructing the past history of human societies and of the human race in general and of defining the laws of progress revealed in it. They did not sufficiently recognize that the philologists and others who used the method to some effect were investigating divergences from a common source, whereas they, for the most part, were not. When, however, they restricted themselves to the development of institutions within a limited range of culturally related societies comparable results were produced, e.g. Maine on the development of Indo-European law, Fustel de Coulanges on the development of early Graeco-Roman religious institutions, and Robertson Smith on the development of Semitic forms of sacrifice; but even so, many of their conclusions were unverifiable. As for the general laws of social development put forward, such as those by McLennan and Morgan, they were not only totally unverifiable but they were largely based on evidences which further research showed to be unsound. Attempts at formulating laws of social progress have now been given up; but not the comparative method, for the very simple reason that it is the only method which, in one form or another, can be employed. What came now to be held by some writers, notably by Radcliffe-Brown in this country, was that, while the method was sound, it had been hitherto used for the wrong purpose. It should be used, not for reconstructing stages of social development, but for the formulation of laws of functional interdependences. However, no such laws have yet been propounded in social anthropology, and until they are it does not seem worth while discussing whether they can be, or what would be their significance if they were. Research directed to this end, at any rate on any scale, has been abandoned in this country, at least for the time being.

Durkheim and his pupils used the comparative method with as much skill and rigour as it is capable of. They were careful to concentrate on a limited range of facts in a limited region and not, like, for instance, McLennan, Frazer and Westermarck, to take them from all over the world, lifting them in the process out of their social setting. The ethnographic data of other regions were used only to see whether the conclusions reached in the area chosen for intensive research had a more general validity or what divergences would have to be accounted for. This is what Durkheim did in his study of Australian totemism, what Hubert and Mauss did in their study of Hindu and Hebrew sacrifice, and what Hertz did in his study of mortuary rites, the core of this study being an analysis of such rites in Indonesia, mostly among the Dayak peoples. In the case of his essay on the right hand he had to cover a wider field, a more extensive survey being both feasible and required in this much less complex topic. This limitation of field is explicitly presented as a methodological principle in 'Le Péché et l'Expiation dans les Sociétés primitives' (p. 37). It would be an erroneous procedure to study sin and expiation by accumulating facts from all over the world and from societies of very diverse types. What is required is an intensive study of a limited and clearly defined cultural region where the facts can be examined in their full contexts of ideas and practices. He chose the Polynesian peoples. Mauss, in an appendix to same essay (p. 59), refers scornfully to those who make collections of facts borrowed indiscriminately from every sort of people and then interpret them superficially by an elementary psychology: association of ideas, scruples, negative magic.[1]

Then, though it is true that Durkheim was attempting to discover causal explanations which have a general validity and might be called laws, he did not conceive of them so naively as did some anthropologists, and his attempt seems to me to have been secondary to an endeavour to relate the facts to one another in such a way that taken together they are intelligible to us both as a whole and singly. Causal explanation is only one kind of understanding. This is, perhaps, more evident in the writings of his pupils and collaborators. In their classical study of magic Hubert and Mauss attempt little more than to show us the fundamental setting and structure of a magic rite, and in their equally fine essay on sacrifice to show us the pattern of sacrificial acts so that we perceive how the whole rite and each part of it make sense. Hertz's essays exemplify this descriptive integration, the meaning of the facts being shown to lie not in themselves, considered as separate facts, but in their interrelation; the art of the anthropologist being to reveal this and hence their meaning. We do not understand what the double disposal of the dead in Indonesia means till we know also the beliefs held about the ghosts of the dead and also about the rules of mourning, but once we have grasped the pattern of these three sides to death—corpse, soul and mourners—we see that each expresses the same idea of transition; and we further understand why a ruler's death cannot be announced, why widows may not be immediately inherited or remarried, why corpses of the very old and of small children are treated differently, etc. Furthermore, we can then make a fruitful comparison

[1] See also Mauss in 'Etude de morphologie sociale', *Année Sociologique*, Vol. IX, 1906, p. 41 and *The Gift*, 1954, pp. 2–3; also Durkheim, *The Elementary Forms of the Religious Life*, n.d., pp. 93–96.

between mortuary rites and other rituals of transition, e.g. initiation and marriage, as both Hertz and Van Gennep did.

The essay on Saint Besse is an attempt by a structural analysis to relate certain prominent and puzzling features of the cult and its attendant myths to local and politico-ecclesiastical organization, thereby rendering them intelligible. This is what I understand by Mauss's insistence on interpretation in terms of 'total social phenomena,' and he shows what he means by that in his essays on seasonal variations of the Eskimos and on gift-exchange. The purpose of the investigation does not go beyond an attempt to discover the essential features of the phenomena studied by relating them to other social phenomena.

These writers are mostly dealing with complexes of ideas. When I said that we are shown the fundamental features of magical, sacrificial, or burial rites the stress should perhaps have been placed on these rites as expressions of conceptions and values. The world of ideas and moral sentiments was the ambient in which these scholars moved, and they were chiefly interested in trying to understand the world of ideas, symbols, and values of primitive men, especially those of a religious and moral order. (A study might be made of this group of French intellectuals, not only the sociologists but Bergson, Proust, and many others, in relation to their dual Jewish and rationalist upbringing and Catholic background.[1]) Ideas and values were not for

[1] Considering that the sociologists among them were agnostics or atheists who believed in some kind of secular neo-Comtian religion of humanity or ritualized system of ethics it might be thought that they would have considered religious subjects not worthy of their first attention. But they had too great an understanding of religion, and they were rationalists too sceptical of rationalism, to take that view. Moreover, they could not fail, given both their own high-minded purpose and the enormous importance they attached to ideals in collective life, to have sympathy, and even admiration, for religious idealism, and in particular for Christian and Jewish faith and teachings. I discuss this point no further than drawing attention to Durkheim's almost obsessive interest in religion and especially his fascination with the idea of *Ecclesia;* to the probability that Mauss's interest in sacrifice began with a like fascination with the drama of the Sacrifice of the Mass, and his interest in prayer (his unfinished essay) with Catholic manuals; and to the origin of

them a mere ideological reflection or superstructure of the
social order. On the contrary, they rather tended to see the
social order as an objective expression of systems of ideas and
values. Lévy-Bruhl, an independent thinker close to the
Durkheimians but whom they never persuaded to join
their, it must be admitted, somewhat doctrinaire group
(another brilliant contemporary writer, Van Gennep, kept,
or was kept, well away from it), paid lip-service to the view
that primitive systems of thought are functions of institutions and vary accordingly, but he never tried to show that,
in fact, this is the case. Having made this formal profession of
faith, he proceeded, and grandly, to examine what really
interested him, the structure of primitive thought as a
virtually independent system of phenomena. Durkheim
himself was also most interested in systems of moral and
religious ideas as an order *sui generis*. No doubt passages, even
many of them, could be cited to the contrary—that is often
the case with a man who has written much and over many
years—but taking Durkheim's writings as a whole, and giving
particular emphasis to those of his maturity, we may agree
with Lévi-Strauss that Durkheim progressively reached the
conclusion that social processes 'belong to the realm of
ideals, and consist essentially of values'.[1] Indeed it would be
difficult not to go further and agree with Dr. Peristiany when
he says: 'Durkheim declares that to explain the function of
ideals by the contribution they make to the maintenance of
the equilibrium, the solidarity or the survival of a society
(as some sociologists tend to do, in the mistaken belief that
they are following Durkheim's teaching) is to misconstrue
the central tenet of his sociology, which assumes that, in
social life, not only are all individuals subordinated to society,
but that society itself is a system of ideas, a system which is
neither an epiphenomenon of social morphology nor an

Hertz's planned great study of sin and pardon which, he makes it very
clear, was his deep interest in the Sacrament of Auricular Confession.
Hertz was very critical of, and indeed, found it difficult not to express
contempt for, what he called 'rationalist theologians', and I think it is
fairly obvious what he meant by that.

[1] Claude Lévi-Strauss, 'French Sociology' in *Twentieth Century
Sociology*, 1945, pp. 508–9.

organ devised to satisfy material needs.'[1] He eschewed mechanical explanations and appeals to inevitability, and to have done otherwise would have run counter to the personal position he took in relation to political and social affairs.[2]

It is, therefore, unfortunate that Durkheim's most quoted affirmation is to the effect that social facts are in some manner to be regarded as 'things' (*des choses*), for 'thing' is certainly not a scientific term but a word of common thought and speech which has the general sense of 'concrete' in contrast to 'abstract'. Its use by Durkheim suggests to the mind that social facts are like objects, whereas what he wished to emphasize was that they are general phenomena and therefore objective. Had he used a word like 'phenomena' instead of 'things' much misunderstanding might have been avoided, as in this typical passage: 'If it is indisputable that the social life is composed exclusively of representations, it in no way follows that an objective science cannot be made of it. The representations of the individual are phenomena equally interior; but, nevertheless, contemporary psychology treats them objectively. Why should it be otherwise with collective representations?'[3]

Above all, Durkheim and his collaborators of the *Année Sociologique* were not economic materialists. His hostility to Marxism is well known. In his treatment of totemism he

[1] Introduction to *Sociology and Philosophy*, pp. xxviii–xxix.

[2] Durkheim was a fervent socialist of the brand of liberal socialism of his time. So also were Lévy-Bruhl, Mauss, and others among his collaborators. I have mentioned earlier Hertz's pamphlet for the Socialist Party. In the same series, which he appears to have founded and organized, were Bianconi's brochure *L'Assistance et les Communes* and Halbwachs' *La Politique foncière des Municipalités*. They were also fervent patriots, and also republicans. Hertz in his brochure advocated certain social reforms which he thought might halt the depopulation of France due to premature deaths and a low birthrate. His what we would call today 'Welfare State' views happened to be in accord in this question with socialist propaganda, but his advocacy was in the interests of all Frenchmen, and it was objective, well-balanced and just. Nevertheless, one cannot help remarking that, in showing how weakness, stupidity and evil are associated with the left side, he did not mention the political connotations of left and right!

[3] In a review of Ch. Seignobos', *La méthode historique appliquée aux sciences sociales* (1901), *Année Sociologique*, Vol. V, 1902, p. 127.

shows the total inadequacy of those who take the view (Haddon, Reuterskioeld, Radcliffe-Brown, Malinowski, and others) that it is to be explained in terms of utility, and he shows, I think conclusively, that the regard paid to the totemic creatures is both secondary and symbolic. On to the creatures are posited conceptions and sentiments derived from elsewhere than from them.[1] We see in Hertz's essay on the right hand the same priority given to ideas and values. The simple, the obvious, explanation, that the organic asymmetry of the two hands lies at the basis of the classification of ideas and values into right and left categories, is rejected, and in its place he maintains that the hands have become the symbols, perhaps in that their slight asymmetry made them suitable for such, of polarities in thought and values because the duality in the universe of ideas must be centred in man who is the centre of them; and that, if the asymmetry cannot be denied, it has been increased often to the point of almost complete disparity, by complexes of ideas and feelings (collective representations) which the hands are made to symbolize.[2] Moreover, once this is understood, the asymmetry is not beyond human control. The left hands of the children of the future can be freed from guilt and inaction.[3] Again, the easy explanation of social procedures after death is horror at the passing, the *rigor mortis*, and the onset of dissolution, but Hertz shows very

[1] Radcliffe-Brown, in what was intended to be a sympathetic interpretation of Durkheim's thought on this topic, made nonsense of it ('The Sociological Theory of Totemism', *Fourth Pacific Science Congress*, Vol. III, 1929). I have had something to say on the question in *Nuer Religion*, 1956, Chaps. III and V.

[2] I am not competent to say whether or to what degree, or even in what sense, there can be said to be an organic asymmetry between the hands. Dr. J. S. Weiner has very kindly given me the gist of some recent papers on the subject, from which I gather that the question is a very complex one, since it is partly a matter of age and situation; but it would appear that the cultural and social element is, as Hertz held, a most important, perhaps the dominant, factor in determining the degree of final disparity.

[3] So, in the socialist pamphlet, whether France was to be saved from extinction was presented as a matter of choice, of will, of conscience—there is nothing here of historical or sociological determinism.

clearly that in many cases there is a minimum of reaction at death, an almost entire lack of concern, so that this cannot be the right interpretation. On the contrary the more repulsive features of dissolution, far from being shunned or secreted, are often emphasized for all to see, for they exhibit objectively the passing of the soul to its happy home. The changing condition of the body signifies changing mental states in the survivors. There is the same preoccupation with sentiments or values, though perhaps less with conceptions, in his fascinating study of the cult of Saint Besse.

Hertz's essays have also still some theoretical interest. Method and theory are not, of course, the same, but it can be said that a method of analysis is of value only if it produces some advance in theory, and that an advance in theory is as important as an exemplification of method as it is in itself. Theory in social anthropology is on a rather low level of abstraction. To avoid entering here into a discussion about it which might lead us far from the limited purpose of this preface, I will take a matter-of-fact position and say that I consider it to be a theoretical contribution to social anthropology when something both new and significant is discovered about some important institution characteristic of primitive societies or primitive societies of a certain type. Even if the facts were known before as separate pieces of information, there is a theoretical advance when they are brought together and shown to be particular instances of a general fact both widespread and important, e.g. exogamy, teknonymy, *rites de passage*, taboo, mana, homeopathic and contagious magic, etc. A theoretical advance can be, and often is, made by intensive study of a single society or social form whereby some essential features of an institution are revealed which are then found to be characteristic of a certain type of society, such as Fustel de Coulanges' analysis of the old Roman, and Robertson Smith's analysis of the old Arabian, lineage system. A theoretical contribution may be couched in terms of historical development, as was Maine's theory of movement in law from status (archaic) to contract (modern). Hertz's contribution in these essays was twofold. It was known, of course, that some peoples have a mortuary ceremony in addition to rites of burial, and even two disposals of the bodily remains, and also that among some peoples right and left have other senses besides those of spatial orientation, but it was not till Hertz brought together and carefully sifted a mass of information bearing on these subjects that it became evident that we are here dealing not with some sporadic and aberrant phenomena but with complexes of phenomena so widely distributed throughout the world that a common origin or borrowing are alike highly improbable, so that they invite general interpretations of a sociological kind.

His second contribution was to provide such interpretations, and they were both new and significant. Whether they are entirely correct is another matter; as everybody knows, a theory may be valuable though eventually it be shown to be inadequate. Certainly they are stimulating hypotheses which can, at least with regard to many points, be put to the test by further research. Unfortunately the essays have remained almost entirely unknown in England and America, the countries from which most anthropological field research has been done, and scarcely any new observations have been made in the light of them, an excellent reason for their publication in an English edition. That is not the author's fault, and it is a misfortune for those who have never read them, for it is nonetheless true, though a commonplace, that one can only make observations relevant to a theory in the light of that theory, for it or against it.

I cannot pretend to go all the way with Hertz. It would be surprising, and not at all to the credit of our discipline, if one could do so fifty years after his essays were written. As I have said, I do not find his fundamental theoretical principle, the dichotomy of sacred and profane, of great value or even very meaningful. I consider his final attribution of secondary mortuary rites to failure of people to adjust themselves, save over a long period of time, to the deaths of their kinsfolk an inadequate interpretation of the facts. But I have found his presentation of the problems and some of his solutions of them most useful in my own research. There are also faults in method. The main one, common to so many anthropological theorists and fatal to their constructions, was to ignore the negative instances. If a general theory is put forward as an explanation of some custom or institution of primitive peoples it must be shown in the terms of that theory how the fact that there are primitive peoples who do not have the custom or institution, or among whom it has a very different character, is to be accounted for. This is a great weakness, it seems to me, in the books and essays of the *Année* group. To take Hertz as an example, what about peoples who do not have secondary disposals of the dead or even secondary mortuary ceremonies? What about those who do not associate opposed values with the two hands? It is true that he does mention the case of the Zuni Indians, among whom the left is regarded as far from inferior to the right, but only to dismiss this awkward case, as Durkheim used to do, as a 'secondary development' (p. 109). Logically, it may appear to be a secondary development but the case would have to rest on historical evidences, which are lacking. A further example is Hertz's emphasis, fortified by what Meillet[1] told him, that in the Indo-European languages the term for right has shown great stability while the terms used for left have shown considerable variability, which suggests that people avoided the word for left, using euphemisms, which in their turn had to be avoided (p. 99). It is true that he instances only the Indo-European languages but an explanation of this sort based on a single instance is no explanation at all. Other examples are necessary if it is to be more than a guess. I have investigated this point in the Nilotic languages of East Africa, spoken by peoples at least some of whom associate a duality of values with the left and right, and I found that there the term for left has been highly stable, as has indeed also the term for right, which shows only phonetic variations in the

---

[1] A. Meillet was the comparative linguist of the *Année* group. That he was primarily a philologist is evident in his discussion of the interplay between particular and common languages, a sociological explanation of change in the meaning of words ('Comment les mots changent de sens', *A.S.* Vol. IX, 1906).

different Nilotic tongues. The tendency Hertz mentions may be peculiar to one culture. One wonders whether it is found frequently, or even at all, among primitives.

There are also general statements which cannot be sustained. That 'primitive thought attributes a sex to all beings in the universe and even to inanimate objects: all of them are divided into two immense classes according to whether they are considered as male or female' (p. 97) would be a most doubtful statement for many primitive peoples. Again, when he says (p. 83) that 'collective thought is primarily concrete and incapable of conceiving a purely spiritual existence' there would be little difficulty in confuting so bald an assertion if it has the meaning it appears to have.[1] Then, would any anthropologist accept today as a general proposition about primitive peoples: 'What more sacred for primitive man than war or the hunt!' (p. 108)?

One feels sometimes in reading these essays a remoteness from the realities of primitive life and this is not to be wondered at, for, like the Master himself, neither Hertz nor, with one exception,[2] any of the group of writers about primitive institutions among Durkheim's collaborators had ever seen a primitive people. This was undoubtedly a disadvantage and was seen by them to have been one; and had it not been for the holocaust of 1914–18 it would doubtless have been overcome. But we must not exaggerate the disadvantage, for it is open to question whether the wide reading a student can undertake during the many years he would have been engaged in carrying out field research and writing it up for publication does not to a considerable degree compensate him for the lack of first-hand experience of primitive peoples. I doubt whether any field anthropologist has made a more important contribution to theory than Davy's study of contract in his *La Foi Jurée* or Bouglé's study of caste (*Essais sur le Régime*

[1] It is much modified in 'La Péché et l'Expiation dans les Sociétés primitives' (p. 34) where he criticises Frazers' conception of the 'naturalistic positivism' of primitives and cites Lévy-Bruhl and Durkheim to show that it is not in accord with the facts.

[2] Henri Beuchat, who died of hunger and cold on a geographical and ethnographical expedition on the Island of Wrangell in 1914.

des Castes),[1] to mention, without particular choice, only two books; and I am convinced that no field study of totemism has excelled Durkheim's analysis. I would even say that no field study of the structure of primitive thought has surpassed in depth and insight the last volumes of Lévy-Bruhl, in spite of his diffuse treatment of the subject. It is a fact, which none can deny, that the theoretical capital on which anthropologists today live is mainly the writings of people whose research was entirely literary, who brought to bear great ability, much learning, and rigorous methods of scholarship on what others had observed and recorded. When that capital is exhausted we are in danger of falling into mere empiricism, one field study after another adding to the number of known facts, but uninspired and uninspiring. If a personal note be allowed, I would, though with serious reservations, identify myself with the *Année* school if a choice had to be made and an intellectual allegiance to be declared.

Had he lived, the young Hertz might have become the equal of his teacher. One day perhaps, Mauss said in mourning his Master and his collaborators, France would replace them. '*Peut-être, la sève reviendra. Une autre graine tombera et germera.*'

---

[1] The introduction to this book has recently been translated and published in English by L. Dumont and D. F. Pocock in *Contributions to Indian Sociology*, no. 2, 1958, pp. 7–30.

THE COLLECTIVE REPRESENTATION
OF DEATH

A CONTRIBUTION
TO THE STUDY OF THE COLLECTIVE
REPRESENTATION OF DEATH*

W E all believe we know what death is because it is a familiar event and one that arouses intense emotion. It seems both ridiculous and sacrilegious to question the value of this intimate knowledge and to wish to apply reason to a subject where only the heart is competent.

Yet questions arise in connection with death which cannot be answered by the heart because the heart is unaware of them. Even for the biologist death is not a simple and obvious fact; it is a problem to be scientifically investigated.[1] But where a human being is concerned the physiological phenomena are not the whole of death. To the organic event is added a complex mass of beliefs, emotions and activities which give it its distinctive character. We see life vanish but we express this fact by the use of a special language: it is the soul, we say, which departs for another world where it will join its forefathers. The body of the deceased is not regarded like the carcass of some animal: specific care must be given to it and a correct burial; not merely for reasons of hygiene but out of moral obligation. Finally, with the occurrence of death a dismal period begins for the living during which special duties are imposed upon them. Whatever their personal feelings may be, they have to show sorrow for a certain period, change the colour of their clothes and modify the pattern of their usual life.

* 'Contribution à une étude sur la représentation collective de la mort', *Année Sociologique*, Vol. X, 1907, pp. 48–137.

Thus death has a specific meaning for the social consciousness; it is the object of a collective representation. This representation is neither simple nor unchangeable: it calls for an analysis of its elements as well as a search for its origin. It is to this double study that we wish to contribute here.

In our own society the generally accepted opinion is that death occurs in one instant. The only purpose of the two or three days' delay between the demise and the burial is to allow material preparations to be made and to summon relatives and friends. No interval separates the life ahead from the one that has just ceased: no sooner has the last breath been exhaled than the soul appears before its judge and prepares to reap the reward for its good deeds or to expiate its sins. After this sudden catastrophe a more or less prolonged period of mourning begins. On certain dates, especially at the 'end of the year,' commemorative ceremonies are held in honour of the deceased. This conception of death, and this particular pattern of events which constitute death and which follow it, are so familiar to us that we can hardly imagine that they are not necessary.

But the facts from many societies less advanced than our own do not fit into this framework. As Lafitau has already pointed out, 'In most primitive societies the dead bodies are only stored, so to speak, in the tomb where they are first placed. After a time they are given a new funeral and they receive the final funerary rites which are due to them.'[2] This difference in custom is not, as we shall see, a mere accident; it brings to light the fact that death has not always been represented and felt as it is in our society.

In the following pages we shall try to establish the complex of beliefs relating to death and practices featuring a double burial. To achieve this aim we shall first use data gathered exclusively from Indonesian peoples, in particular the

Dayak[3] of Borneo,* among whom this phenomenon takes a typical form. We shall then show, on the basis of sources relating to other ethnographic areas, that these are not merely local customs. In our account we shall follow the sequence of the events themselves, dealing first with the period between the death (in the usual sense of the word) and the final obsequies, and then with the concluding ceremony.

1. THE INTERMEDIARY PERIOD

The ideas and practices occasioned by death can be classified under three headings, according to whether they concern the body of the deceased, his soul, or the survivors. This distinction does not by any means have an absolute value, but it does facilitate the presentation of the facts.

(a) The body: provisional burial

Among peoples of the Malay archipelago who have not yet been too deeply influenced by foreign cultures it is the custom not to take the body at once to its final burial place; this move can only be made after a more or less long period of time during which the body is placed in a temporary shelter.

The general rule, among the Dayak, seems to have been to keep the bodies of chiefs and of wealthy people inside their own houses till the time of the final burial. The body is then put in a coffin the cracks of which are sealed with a resinous substance.[4] The Dutch Government forbade this practice, at least in certain districts, for hygienic reasons; but quite different reasons besides that of foreign interference must have limited the extent of this kind of temporary burial. The living owe all kinds of care

* ['Dayak' is not the name of any particular Bornean people. It derives from *dayah*, a word common to middle Borneo languages, meaning simply 'upriver'. It is used, especially by Dutch ethnographers, to designate generally the indigenous peoples of the interior. The Dayak discussed by Hertz are mainly the Olo Ngaju, a large cultural grouping of riverine peoples in southeastern Borneo. *Ngaju* itself also means 'upriver'; *olo*, 'man'.—R. N.]

to the dead who reside among them. There is an uninter-
rupted wake which, as in Ireland or among our own farmers,
entails much upheaval and great expenses,[5] but for a much
longer period. Furthermore, the presence of a corpse in the
house imposes taboos on the inhabitants which are often
severe: an inconvenience which is strongly felt because the
Dayak longhouse is frequently the whole village in itself.[6]
It is for these reasons that the prolonged exposure of the
body is nowadays exceptional.

As for those deceased who do not seem to deserve such
heavy sacrifices, a shelter is provided by laying the coffin,
after it has been exposed for a few days, either in a miniature
wooden house raised on piles[7] or, more often, on a kind of
platform simply covered by a roof.[8] This temporary burial
place is sometimes in the immediate neighbourhood of the
deceased person's house, but more often it is in a deserted
place in the depth of the forest.[9] Thus, if the deceased no
longer has a place in the big house of the living, he at least
possesses his own little house, one which is almost identical
with those[10] temporarily occupied by Dayak families when
the cultivation of rice forces them to scatter over an area
which is often very extensive.[11]

This type of temporary burial, although apparently
the most common one in the Malay archipelago, is not the
only one that exists there; it may even be derived from a
more ancient one which we find mentioned in several
places:[12] the exposure of the corpse, wrapped in bark, in
the branches of a tree. On the other hand, instead of ex-
posing the coffin to the atmosphere it is often preferred to
bury it fairly deep, even though this means digging it up
later.[13] Whatever the variety of these customs, which often
co-exist in one place and are substituted one for the other,
the rite, in its essence, is constant; the body of the deceased,
while awaiting the second burial, is temporarily deposited
in a burial-place distinct from the final one; it is almost
invariably isolated.

This period of waiting varies in length. To take only the Olo Ngaju as an example, some authors mention a delay of seven to eight months or a year between the time of death and the celebration of the final ceremony called *tivah*;[14] but this, according to Hardeland,[15] is a minimum to which the period is only rarely limited; the usual delay is about two years and is often exceeded; in many cases four or six,[16] or even ten[17] years elapse before the last homage is paid to the deceased.[18] This abnormal postponement of a rite which is as necessary to the peace and the well-being of the survivors as it is to the salvation of the deceased, is explained by the magnitude of the feast which has to accompany this rite. The feast involves very complicated material preparations which in themselves often require a year or even more;[19] it assumes considerable resources in money as well as in goods (sacrificial victims, food, drink, etc.) which are seldom available and have first to be accumulated by the relatives. Furthermore, an ancient custom, still practised by many tribes of the interior, forbids the celebration of the *tivah* till a newly-taken human head has been acquired; and this takes time, especially since the bothersome interference of Europeans. Yet, if these exterior causes account for the long delays which often occur in the celebration of the *tivah*, they are not sufficient[20] to explain the necessity of a period of waiting and to fix its length. Even if all the necessary material conditions for the final burial were fulfilled, it could still not take place immediately after the death: the right thing to do is to wait for the corpse to have completely decomposed till only the bones remain.[21] With the Olo Ngaju and some other Indonesian peoples, this pattern is not apparent because of the extreme magnitude of their funerary feast, and because of the long and expensive preparations it requires.[22] But in other tribes the obligation to wait until the bones are dry before proceeding with the final rites is, without any doubt, the direct cause of the period of delay and determines its length.[23] We are thus justified in believing that, normally, the time which elapses between the occurrence of death and the final ceremony corresponds to the time judged necessary for the corpse to reach a skeletal condition, but that there are secondary reasons which arise and so prolong this period, sometimes indefinitely.

The fact that the state of the corpse has an influence upon the final rites is clearly shown by the care the survivors take in hermetically sealing all cracks in the coffin and in ensuring the flow of putrid matters to the exterior, either by draining them into the ground or by collecting them in an earthenware vessel.[24] This is not a matter of hygiene (as we understand the word) nor even, exclusively, a concern to ward off foul smells: we must not attribute to these peoples feelings and scruples about smell which are foreign to them.[25] An expression uttered several times in the course of a *tivah* shows us the true reason for these practices: the putrefaction of the corpse is assimilated to 'the petrifying thunderbolt' because it too threatens with sudden death the members of the house which it strikes.[26] The reason they consider it so highly desirable that the putrefaction should take place in a sealed container is that the evil power which resides in the corpse and which is linked with the smells must not be allowed to escape and strike the living.[27] On the other hand they do not want the putrid matter to remain inside the coffin, because as the desiccation of his bones progresses so the deceased himself must be gradually freed from the mortuary infection.[28]

The mystical importance which the Indonesians attach to the disintegration of the body is also seen in the practices connected with the products of the decomposition. With the Olo Ngaju, the pot in which they have been collected is broken at the second funeral and its fragments are laid in the final burial-place with the bones.[29] The Olo Maanyan usage is more significant: when the corpse is kept in the house, on the forty-ninth day after death the pot is detached and the contents are examined: 'If it contains too much matter, a penalty is inflicted,[30] the relatives (of the deceased) have not done their duty.' The container is again carefully attached to the coffin and these remain together in the house till the final ceremony.[31] This custom is clearly only a survival: to discern its former significance we need only compare it with customs observed in other parts of the Malay Archipelago. In Bali, though this island has been deeply influenced by Hinduism, the custom is to keep the body in the house for many weeks before cremating it: the coffin is pierced at the bottom 'to permit the escape of the liquids, which are gathered in a basin that is emptied every day with great ceremony'.[32] Finally, in Borneo itself the Dayak of the Kapuas collect in earthenware dishes the liquids produced by the decomposition and mix them with the rice which the close relatives eat during the period of mourning.[33] It would be better not to interpret these customs for the moment as we shall meet them again more widespread and in a more complex form outside the area we are studying; let us conclude provisionally that the Indonesians attach a particular importance to the changes that occur in the corpse; their ideas in this matter prevent them from terminating the funeral rites at once and impose specific precautions and observances on the survivors.

So long as the final rite has not been celebrated the corpse is exposed to grave perils. It is a belief familiar to anthropologists and folklorists that the body is at certain times particularly exposed to the attacks of evil spirits and to all the harmful influences by which man is threatened;[34] its diminished powers of resistance have to be reinforced by magical means. The period which follows death is particularly dangerous in this respect; that is why the corpse must be exorcised and be forearmed against demons. This preoccupation inspires, at least partly, the ablutions and various rites connected with the body immediately after death: such as, for instance, the custom of closing the eyes and other orifices of the body with coins or beads;[35] it also imposes on the survivors the duty of keeping the deceased company during this dreaded period, to keep watch by his side and to beat gongs frequently in order to keep malignant spirits at bay.[36] Thus the corpse, afflicted by a special infirmity, is an object of solicitude for the survivors at the same time as an object of fear.

(b) *The soul: its temporary stay on earth*

In the same way as the body is not taken at once to its 'last resting-place', so the soul does not reach its final destination immediately after death. It must first undergo a kind of probation, during which it stays on earth in the proximity of the body, wandering in the forest or frequenting the places it inhabited while it was alive: it is only at the end of this period, at the time of the second funeral, and thanks to a special ceremony, that it will enter the land of the dead. This at least is the simplest form taken by this belief.[37]

But the ideas relating to the fate of the soul are in their very nature vague and indefinite; we should not try to make them too clear-cut. In fact, the opinion most common among the Olo Ngaju[38] is more complex: at the moment of death the soul splits into two parts, the *salumpok liau*, which is 'the marrow of the soul', the essential element of the personality, and the *liau krahang* or corporeal soul, compounded of the souls of the bones, hair, nails, etc.;[39] the latter, unconscious and as though benumbed, remains with the corpse until the *tivah*; as for the soul proper, it continues to live, but its life is somewhat unstable.[40] Undoubtedly it reaches the celestial 'city of souls' the very day after death; but it does not yet have an appointed place there; it does not feel at ease in these lofty regions; it is sad and as though lost, and pines for its other half. That is why it often escapes and returns to wander about on earth and to watch over the coffin that holds its body. The great final feast must be celebrated if the soul, solemnly admitted to the land of the dead and rejoined by the *liau krahang*, is to regain a secure and substantial existence.[41]

Similarly, among the Alfuru of central Celebes there is the belief that the soul remains on earth by the side of the body till the final ceremony (*tengke*); but the most common belief is that the soul goes to the underworld immediately after death: it cannot, however, enter the communal home of souls at once; it must live outside it, in a separate house, till the celebration of the *tengke*. The meaning of this idea appears clearly if we compare it with a custom observed among the same tribes: the parents of a dead child sometimes wish to keep its body with them (instead of burying it); in this case they may not continue to live in the village but must build a house for themselves isolated at some distance. Thus these tribes attribute their own feelings to the souls of the other world; and the presence of a dead person during the period preceding the final funeral can no more be tolerated in the village of the living than in that of the dead. The reason for this temporary exclusion is explicitly stated: it is that 'Lamoa (God) cannot stand the stench of corpses.' Although this statement may contain some element of foreign origin, the idea that it expresses is certainly indigenous: it is only when the decomposition of the corpse is completed that the newcomer among the dead is thought to be rid of his impurity and deemed worthy of admittance to the company of his ancestors.[42]

However, in some tribes the priests celebrate a ceremony, soon after the death has occurred, which conducts the soul to the other world;[43] but even in such a case it does not fully enter its new life. In the beginning it is not fully aware that it has left this world; its home is dark and unpleasant; it is frequently forced to return to earth in search of food which it is denied there. The survivors must ameliorate this painful situation by certain observances, in particular by the offering of a human head; but it is only after the final ceremony that the soul will be able to provide for itself and taste fully the joys that the land of the dead has to offer.[44]

Thus, in spite of apparent contradictions, the soul never suddenly severs the ties which bind it to its body and which hold it back on earth. As long as the temporary burial of the corpse lasts[45] the deceased continues to belong more or less exclusively to the world he has just left. To the living falls the duty of providing for him: twice a day till the final ceremony, the Olo Maanyan bring him his usual meal;[46] besides, when it is neglected the soul knows very well how to take its share of rice and drink.[47] During the whole of this period the deceased is looked upon as having not yet completely ended his earthly existence: this is so true that in Timor, when a Rajah dies, his successor cannot be officially named until the corpse has had its final burial; for until that burial the deceased is not truly dead, he is simply 'asleep in his house'.[48]

But if it is true that this period of transition prolongs the soul's previous existence, it does so in a precarious and lugubrious manner. The stay of the soul among the living is somewhat illegitimate and clandestine. It lives, as it were, marginally in the two worlds: if it ventures into the afterworld, it is treated there like an intruder; here on earth it is an importunate guest whose proximity is dreaded. As it has no resting place it is doomed to wander incessantly, waiting anxiously for the feast which will put an end to its restlessness.[49] It is thus not surprising that during this period the soul should be considered as a malicious being: it finds the solitude into which it has been thrust hard to bear and tries to drag the living with it.[50] Not yet having regular means of subsistence such as the dead are provided with, it has to pilfer from its relatives; in its present distress it remembers all the wrongs it has suffered during its life and seeks revenge.[51] It watches its relatives' mourning sharply and if they do not properly fulfil their duties towards itself, if they do not actively prepare its release, it becomes irritated and inflicts diseases upon them,[52] for death has endowed it with magical powers which enable it to put its bad intentions into practice. Whilst later, when it has its place among the dead, it will only visit its relatives when expressly invited, now it 'returns' of its own initiative through necessity or through malice, and its untimely appearance spreads terror.[53]

This state of the soul, both pitiful and dangerous, during this confused period explains the complex attitude of the living in which pity and fear are mixed in variable proportions.[54] They try to provide for the needs of the deceased and to ease his condition; but at the same time they remain on the defensive and refrain from contacts which they know to be harmful. When, the very next day after death, they have the soul led into the world of the dead, it is not known whether they are motivated by the hope of sparing the soul a painful wait, or by the desire to rid themselves as quickly as possible of its sinister presence; in fact both these preoccupations are mingled in their consciousness.[55] These fears of the living can only end completely when the soul has lost the painful and disquieting character that it has after the death.

(c) The living: mourning

Not only are the relatives of the deceased compelled to devote all kinds of care towards him during the intermediary period, not only are they the target of the spite and sometimes the attacks of the tormented soul, but they are moreover subjected to a whole set of prohibitions which constitute the mourning.[56] Death, in fact, by striking the individual, has given him a new character; his body, which (except in certain abnormal cases) was in the realm of the ordinary, suddenly leaves it; it can no longer be touched without danger, it is an object of horror and dread. Now we know to what degree the religious or magical properties of things are regarded as contagious by 'primitives': the 'impure cloud'[57] which, according to the Olo Ngaju, surrounds the deceased, pollutes everything it touches; i.e. not only the people and objects that have been in physical contact with the corpse, but also everything that is intimately connected, in the minds of the survivors, with the image of the deceased. His belongings may no longer be used for profane purposes; they must be destroyed or dedicated to the deceased, or at least stripped, by appropriate rites, of the harmful quality they have acquired. Similarly, the fruit trees that belonged to the deceased, and the streams where he used to fish, are the objects of a strict taboo; if the fruit and fish are taken they are used exclusively as provisions for the great funeral feast.[58] The house of the deceased is impure for a more or less long period and the river on the bank of which it is built is tabooed.[59]

As for the relatives of the deceased, they feel in themselves the blow that has struck one of them: a ban separates them from the rest of the community. They may not leave their village nor pay any visits; those most directly affected sometimes spend whole months confined to a corner of their house, sitting motionless and doing nothing. Neither may they receive visitors from outside, nor (should this be allowed) may they answer when they are questioned.[60] They are forsaken, not only by men but also by the protective spirits: as long as their impurity lasts they cannot hope for any help from the powers above.[61] The ban which is imposed on them affects their entire way of life. In consequence of the funerary contagion they are changed, and set apart from the rest of humanity; therefore they can no longer live the way others do. They may not share the diet nor follow the ways of dressing or adornment or of arranging the hair which are proper to individuals who are socially normal and which are the sign of this community to which (for a time) they no longer belong;[62] hence the numerous taboos and special prescriptions to which people in mourning must conform.[63]

Although the funeral pollution extends to all the relatives of the deceased and to all the inhabitants of the house where the death occurred, they are not all equally affected: thus the length of the mourning varies necessarily according to the degree of kinship. Among the Olo Ngaju, distant relatives are impure only for the few days[64] immediately following the death; then, after a ceremony during which several hens are sacrificed, they may resume their ordinary life.[65] But as for the closer relatives of the deceased,[66] the particular condition which affects them is not dissipated so quickly or so easily; a long time must elapse before they can be completely freed of the ban that weighs upon them, a period which coincides precisely with the length of the temporary sepulture. During this period they must observe the taboos imposed on them by their state. A widower or a widow has no right to remarry, because the tie that binds the surviving spouse to the deceased will only be severed by the final ceremony.[67] Indeed the close relatives, because they are as it were one with the deceased, share his condition, are included with him in the feelings which he inspires in the community, and are subject, like him, to a taboo during the whole interval between the death and the second funeral.

The facts do not always have the typical simplicity which we find, for instance, among the Olo Ngaju. The delay, often very long, necessitated by the preparations for the burial feast would prolong almost indefinitely the privations and hardships of mourning if the adoption of a fixed and relatively close date did not remedy this situation.[68] It is very likely—though this fact cannot, it appears, be historically proved for the societies we are dealing with—that such a shortening of the mourning-period has occurred fairly frequently. Moreover, as Wilken has shown,[69] the new date, set to mark the end of mourning instead of the final burial, need not have been chosen arbitrarily. Indeed, the state of the deceased during the intermediary period is not immutable: he undergoes changes which gradually weaken the dangerous character of the corpse and the soul and which compel the living, at certain dates, to hold special ceremonies. These dates, which at first constituted for the mourners merely stages towards liberation, have later become the time marking the end of their impurity. In this way compulsory mourning expires among the Olo Maanyan at the ceremony of the forty-ninth day[70] and not, as among the Olo Ngaju, at the time of the final feast.

On the other hand, according to many sources, the lifting of the mourning-taboos coincides with the acquisition of a human head by the relatives of the deceased, and with the ceremony that takes place on the occasion of this happy event.[71] But this custom too seems to be of an evolution whose principal stages we can determine. Among the Olo Ngaju the sacrifice of a human victim (whose head is cut off) is, as we shall see, one of the essential acts of the funeral feast.[72] Sacrifice is indeed an indispensable condition for the conclusion of the mourning-period, but it is part of a complex whole and is bound up with the final burial. Among the Sea Dayak of Sarawak this rite assumes an autonomous character; certainly the *ulit* or taboo which constitutes the mourning ends completely only with the feast for the deceased. 'However, if in the meantime a human head has been acquired and celebrated in the village, the taboos are partially lifted and the wearing of ornaments is allowed again.'[73] Should this procedure continue, and the practice of double burial be abandoned,[74] a successful 'head-hunt', a partly fortuitous event and in any case external to the state of the deceased, will be enough to assure the release of the survivors.

Thus the long mourning of the relatives among these Indonesians seems to be bound up with ideas about the body and the soul of the deceased during the intermediary period; this mourning lasts normally till the second burial. Divergent customs in which this relationship is not apparent are due, we believe, to a later relaxation of the original custom.

The idea that the last funeral rites may not be celebrated immediately after death but only at the end of a certain period is not at all peculiar to the Indonesians nor to any one particular race;[75] this is proved by the fact that the custom of temporary burial is extremely common.

Certainly the special forms which this custom takes are extremely varied; and it is very likely that ethnic and geographical reasons contribute to the predominance of a certain kind of temporary disposal of the body in a given cultural area,[76] but that is a separate problem which we do not intend to discuss here. From our point of view there is a strict similarity between the exposure of the corpse in the branches of a tree, as is practised by tribes of Central Australia,[77] or inside the house of the living, as is found among certain Papuans[78] and among some Bantu[79] tribes, or on a platform specially raised, as is usually done by the Polynesians[80] and by many Indian tribes of North America,[81] or lastly the temporary burial chiefly practised by South American Indians.[82] All these various forms of temporary burial, which in a technical classification would probably have to appear under separate headings, are equivalent for us. They all have the same object, namely to offer the deceased a temporary residence until the natural disintegration of the body is completed and only the bones remain.

But certain funeral customs cannot, it seems, be reduced to this general type: the aim of embalmment is precisely to prevent the corruption of the flesh and the transformation of the body into a skeleton; cremation on the other hand forestalls the spontaneous alteration of the corpse with a rapid and almost complete destruction. We believe that these artificial ways of disposal do not differ essentially from the temporary ways that we have listed. The complete demonstration of this thesis would lead us too far from our subject;

it must be enough for us merely to indicate here briefly
the reasons which justify it in our eyes.

Let us first note that mummification is in certain cases a
mere result of temporary exposure or burial, due to the
desiccating qualities of the soil or of the air.[83] Furthermore,
even when the survivors do not intend to preserve the corpse
artificially, they do not always abandon it completely
during its decomposition. Since the transformation which it
undergoes is painful and dangerous for itself as well as for
those who surround it, steps are often taken to shorten the
putrefaction, to diminish its intensity or to neutralize its
sinister effects. A fire is kept burning beside the deceased in
order to keep malign influences at bay, and also to warm the
wandering soul and to exercise a soothing action upon the
body,[84] which is surrounded by scented smoke and smeared
with aromatic ointments.[85] The transition from these
customs to the practice of smoking the corpse on a wicker-
work frame[86] or to a rudimentary embalmment[87] is almost
imperceptible. To pass from the spontaneous desiccation,
which leaves only the bones, to the special form of desiccation which transforms the corpse into a mummy, it is
enough for the survivors to have developed a desire to
consign to the final grave a body as little changed as possible.[88] In this the Egyptian funeral ritual agrees essentially
with the beliefs and practices of the Indonesians: for seventy
days, the embalmer fights the corruption which tries to
invade the corpse; it is only at the end of this period that the
body, having become imperishable, is taken to the grave,
that the soul departs for the fields of Ialu and that the
mourning of the survivors comes to an end.[89] It seems legitimate therefore to consider mummification as a special
case derived from temporary burial.

As for cremation,[90] it is usually neither a final act, nor
sufficient in itself; it calls for a later and complementary
rite. In ancient Indian ritual, for instance, what is left of
the body after it has been burnt must be carefully collected,

as are the ashes, and deposited at the end of a certain period in a funeral monument;[91] the cremation, and the burial of the burned bones, correspond respectively to the first and the second burial among the Indonesians.[92] Evidently the very nature of the rite that is performed renders indeterminate the interval between the initial ceremony and the final one. This interval may be reduced to such an extent that both ceremonies form a single continuous whole,[93] which does not, however, prevent the cremation being a preliminary operation and occupying, within the system of funeral rites, the same place as the temporary exposure.[94] To this external similarity corresponds moreover a deeper resemblance: the immediate purpose of the temporary burial is, as we shall see, to give the bones time to dry completely. This transformation is not, in the eyes of the 'primitives', a mere physical disintegration; it changes the character of the corpse, turns it into a new body, and is, consequently, a necessary condition for the salvation of the soul. This is precisely the meaning of cremation: far from destroying the body of the deceased, it recreates it and makes it capable of entering a new life;[95] it thus achieves the same result as the temporary exposure,[96] but in a much faster way.[97] The violent action of the fire spares the dead and the living the sorrows and dangers involved in the transformation of the corpse; or at least, it shortens that period considerably by accomplishing all at once the destruction of the flesh[98] and the reduction of the body to immutable elements which in nature happens slowly and progressively.[99] Thus there is a difference of duration and of means between cremation and the various modes of temporary sepulture, but not a difference of kind.

In all the rites studied so far, the soft parts of the corpse, where they are not preserved by artificial means, are purely and simply destroyed: they are looked upon as mere perishable and impure elements from which the bones must be separated; but more complex representations come to light in the practice known as endocannibalism,[100] which consists in the ritual consumption of the deceased person's flesh by his relatives. This custom obviously does not have as exclusive aim the purification of the bones. It is not a refined cruelty like normal cannibalism, nor the fulfilment of a physical appetite; it is a sacred meal of which only certain definite groups of the tribe's members[101] can partake and from which the women, among the Binbinga at least, are strictly excluded. By this rite the living incorporate into their own being the vitality and the special qualities residing in the flesh of the deceased; if this flesh were allowed to dissolve, the community would lose strength to which it is entitled.[102] But, at the same time, endocannibalism spares the deceased the horror of a slow and vile decomposition, and allows his bones to reach their final state almost immediately. Furthermore, it secures for the flesh the most honourable of sepultures.[103] In any case, the existence of this practice does not essentially alter the general type that we are trying to set up here, since after the consumption of the flesh the bones are gathered and kept by the relatives of the deceased for a certain period, at the end of which the final funeral is celebrated. During this period the soul is supposed to prowl around the bones and the sacred fire which is kept burning nearby, and silence is strictly imposed on close relatives of the deceased.[104] Thus, endocannibalism, whatever its direct causes might be, takes its place among the various practices observed in order to lay bare the bones in the intermediary period between death and the last funeral rites.

We have seen that the period of waiting coincides in a great many cases with the real or presumed duration of the decomposition; it is usually over the dried and almost unchangeable remains that the last funeral rites are celebrated. It thus seems natural to suppose that there is a relation between the institution of the temporary funeral and the representations engendered by the dissolution of the corpse: it is unthinkable to give the deceased his final burial while he is still immersed in infection.[105] The interpretation is not a gratuitous hypothesis: we find it presented as an essential dogma all through the *Zend-Avesta*. For the followers of Mazdaism, a corpse is the impure object *par excellence*,[106] and innumerable rules aim at preserving from funeral contagion the people and things belonging to the good creation. It is an assault upon the sanctity of earth, water and fire to inflict upon them the foul contact of a dead body:[107] the corpse must be banished to some distant and sterile height and, if possible, inside a stone enclosure[108] 'where carnivorous dogs and birds are known to come'.[109] Vultures and wild beasts, the Parsi believe, are the great purifiers of the corpse, because it is in the corruptible flesh that lives the *Nasu*, the devilish infection. A year later, when the bones are completely bared and dry, the soil on which they lie will be pure[110] and they may be touched, as is explicitly stated by Ormazd, without pollution.[111] This will be the time to lay them in an ossuary, their final tomb.[112] Thus in Zoroastrianism the function of the temporary exposure is to isolate the corpse, which is considered dangerous, and at the same time to ensure its purification. But perhaps the Avestan texts only show us the product of a subtle and later theological reflection: we must discover what meaning younger societies attach to reducing the body to a skeleton.

Indonesian sources have allowed us to see a kind of symmetry or parallelism between the condition of the body, which has to wait a certain time before it can enter its final tomb, and the condition of the soul, which will be properly admitted into the land of the dead only when the last funeral rites are accomplished; but in other ethnographic areas these two groups of facts are more directly linked. Certain Caribs of French Guiana put the deceased temporarily in a pit, on a seat with all his ornaments and his weapons: they bring him food and drink till the bones are completely denuded because, they say, the dead 'do not go up there till they are fleshless'.[113] In the same way, among the Botocudo, the soul remains in the neighbourhood of the tomb till the decomposition is completed; and during all this time it worries the living who happen to approach it.[114] These tribes thus explicitly connect the dissolution of the corpse and their belief in a temporary stay of the soul on earth, together with the obligations and fears that derive from this belief.

It is not arbitrarily that they delay the final departure of the soul in this manner until the body is completely decomposed. This representation is linked to a well-known belief: to make a material object or a living being pass from this world into the next, to free or to create the soul, it must be destroyed. The destruction may be sudden, as in sacrifice, or slow as in the gradual wearing-away of the consecrated objects deposited in a sacred place or on the tomb. As the visible object vanishes it is reconstructed in the beyond, transformed to a greater or lesser degree.[115] The same belief applies to the soul and body of the deceased. According to the Ainu, 'death is not the matter of a moment'; so long as the decomposition is not ended, life and soul subsist to some extent inside or near the tomb: 'the soul frees itself gradually from its earthly tabernacle' and one must be careful to leave it alone during all this time.[116] An identical idea is found, with more details, in a certain tribe of north-west America: as the dissolution of the corpse progresses so the souls of those who have died before come every night and remove the flesh from the bones and carry it to the house of the souls, located at the centre of the earth; when this operation is completed the deceased possesses a new body similar to the old one, except for the fact that the bones have remained on earth.[117]

But beside this spiritual duplicate of his body, man possesses another soul, which is mobile and relatively independent. During its life on earth this soul, which was

already capable of leaving the body occasionally and of
existing on its own, can live an independent life immediately
after the death; moreover, it is precisely its departure which
causes the body to disintegrate. However, the former solidarity persists; if the soul reaches the land of the dead at
once, it nevertheless feels the effect of the body's condition.
In several Melanesian islands it is believed that the soul
remains weak for as long as the putrefaction lasts; after
its arrival in the other world it stays still at first; the magical
powers that it possesses are temporarily torpid. When every
trace of the smell has disappeared the soul regains its strength
and activity enhanced, it becomes a *tindalo*, a protective
spirit which the living will worship; 'it has ceased to be a
man.'[118] Perhaps we should take this last statement literally
since the spirits of the dead in Melanesia, at least a great
many of them, are often supposed to live in the bodies of
various animals, in particular of sharks and frigate-birds.[119]
Death is fully consummated only when decomposition has
ended; only then does the deceased cease to belong to this
world so as to enter another life.

It is not surprising that similar ideas are found in
Madagascar, since the peoples of that island are related to
the Indonesians. The Sihanaka believe that while the flesh
detaches from the bones, the soul experiences bitter sufferings:
if it succeeds in overcoming them, it will continue to live
as a spirit indefinitely; but if it succumbs it has to enter the
body of a butterfly.[120] Maybe a foreign element has been
grafted here upon the original idea: it is none the less
remarkable that the intermediary period should be considered as a time of ordeals and that the soul's sufferings
should be linked to the transformation which goes on in
the body. But the most common belief among the Malagasy
is that the liquids resulting from the decomposition of the
flesh give birth to some more or less mythical animal which
is none other than the new incarnation of the soul; that
is why these liquids are carefully collected in earthenware

jugs; sometimes they are sprinkled with ox-blood to make more certain the rebirth of the deceased. Among the Betsileo it is forbidden to give the remains a burial or to work in the fields so long as the deceased has not 'returned' in the form of a small worm.[121] It is always the same notion which reappears in various forms: the dissolution of the former body conditions and prepares the formation of the new body which the soul will henceforth inhabit.

We must beware of attributing to the various representations a generality and an explanatory value which they do not have. It would be arbitrary to elevate such and such a particular belief into a universal truth; to affirm for instance that the new body of the deceased is always formed by his volatised flesh.[122] In fact, as we shall see, the bones are often thought to be the material support of the disincarnated soul. These opposed concepts agree in their essential point; in different ways they express a constant theme. Two complementary notions seem to compose this theme. The first is that death is not completed in one instantaneous act; it implies a lasting procedure which, at least in a great many instances, is considered terminated only when the dissolution of the body has ended. The second is that death is not a mere destruction but a transition: as it progresses so does the rebirth; while the old body falls to ruins, a new body takes shape, with which the soul—provided the necessary rites have been performed—will enter another existence, often superior to the previous one.

During this entire period when death is not yet completed, the deceased is treated as if he were still alive: food is brought to him, his relatives and friends keep him company and speak to him.[123] He retains all his rights over his wife and guards them jealously. The widow is literally the wife of a person in whom death is present and continuous; thus she is considered during that period as impure and accursed and is condemned in a great many societies to the abject existence of an outcast; it is only at the time of the final ceremony that she can be freed and allowed by the kin of the deceased either to re-marry or to return to her family.[124] In the same way, the inheritance sometimes remains intact till the day the deceased has truly left this world.[125] But the most instructive facts are those concerning the succession of kings and chiefs.

The custom of not proclaiming the successor to a chief until the final ceremony, a custom which we had already encountered in Timor, is reported from several peoples belonging to different ethnic groups.[126] We may imagine the dangers of such an interregnum to the societies which are subjected to it. The death of a chief causes a deep disturbance in the social body which, especially if it is prolonged, has weighty consequences. It often seems that the blow which strikes the head of the community in the sacred person of the chief has the effect of suspending temporarily the moral and political laws and of setting free the passions which are nor-mally kept in check by the social order.[127] Thus we often en-counter the custom of keeping the death of the chief secret during a period varying in length; those closest to the deceased are the only ones to know the truth, and they rule in his name; for others, the chief is merely ill.[128] In Fiji, the secret is kept for a period varying between four and ten days; then, when the subjects, who begin to suspect some-thing and who are impatient to be able legitimately to pillage and destroy, come to ask whether the chief has died, they are told that 'his body is decomposed by now'. It only remains for the disappointed visitors to go away; they have come too late and have missed their opportunity. The idea at work here, adds the author who reports these facts, is that so long as the decomposition is not sufficiently advanced, one is not really finished with the deceased, and his authority cannot be transmitted to his successor: the hand of the deceased can no longer hold the sceptre, but it has not yet let go.[129] One must wait for the King to be entirely dead before one can cry: Long live the King!

If time is necessary for death to be completed, so also

D

the evil energies which it sets to work will not exhaust their effects in a moment; they are present in the heart of the living community and threaten to make new victims there. Of course, certain rites can to some extent attenuate the dangerous impurity of the corpse:[130] but it nevertheless remains the permanent centre of a contagious infection. From the temporary sepulture spreads a harmful influence[131] which makes the living stay away. The fear inspired by the proximity of death is so intense that it often causes actual migrations: in the Andaman Islands for instance, the natives, after burying the deceased, desert the village and go and camp far away in temporary shelters; they do not return to their normal homes till some months later when the time has come to hold the final ceremony.[132] The taboo which affects the individual while death is at work in him is communicated not only to the place where he happens to be but also to the objects which have belonged to him: in various Melanesian islands one must not touch the canoe of the deceased, his trees, or his dog until the final burial has lifted the death-taboo.[133]

The institution of mourning[134] is to be linked to the same ideas. If the funeral impurity is prolonged for a definite time it is because death itself goes on till the performance of the last rites and because a close and obligatory solidarity unites certain of the survivors and the deceased. Even more than is apparent from Indonesian data, there exists an internal connection between the condition of the deceased and that of his close relatives during the intermediary phase.[135] This is clearly illustrated by a Maori tradition which quotes the last words of a chief to his son. 'For three years', he tells him, 'your person must be sacred and you must remain apart from the tribe . . . for during all that time my hands will gather earth and my mouth will feed constantly on worms and vile food, the only kind that is offered to the spirits in the underworld. Then, when my head falls upon my body and when the fourth year has come, waken me from my sleep, show my face to the light of day. When I arise, you will be *noa*, free.'[136] Thus mourning is merely the direct consequence in the living of the actual state of the deceased.[137]

The solidarity which unites the deceased to his nearest relatives is expressed in certain societies by customs some of which we have met among Indonesians. These relatives, especially the widow, are compelled either daily or at fixed dates, to collect the liquid produced by the decomposition of the flesh, in order to smear it on to their own body or to mix it into their food.[138] Those who observe such practices justify them by alleging their affection for the deceased and the sorrow they feel at having lost him. But these motives are not enough to account for the rite; this is often compulsory; the women on whom this duty falls are threatened with capital punishment if they do not comply.[139] It is thus not simply a question of the spontaneous expression of an individual feeling but of a forced participation of certain survivors in the present condition of the deceased. Death must be given its due if it is not to continue its ravages within the group. In communicating after a fashion with the deceased the living make themselves immune and spare the afflicted community fresh misfortunes. Sometimes they hope to assimilate in this way the qualities of the deceased,[140] or to absorb the mystical power residing in the corpse.[141] Whether through duty or through self-interest, these people live in an intimate and continuous contact with death; and the community of the living rejects them from its midst.[142]

This exclusion does not necessarily suppose a material contact of the living with the corpse. So long as death is at work, the immediate family of the deceased are targets for 'the mysterious action of hostile forces'. In less civilised societies there is no clear distinction between misfortune and impurity: the affliction of the mourners pollutes them profoundly.[143] Their physical integrity itself is impaired;

their body is hardly distinguishable from the corpse. 'People are disgusted by my body', says a Hupa in mourning. 'That is why I do not have my fire where they have theirs; do not eat what others eat; do not look at people since my body frightens them so.'[144] They are truly 'people of death'.[145] They live in darkness,[146] dead themselves from a social point of view, because any active participation on their part in collective life would only spread abroad the curse they carry in them.[147]

We have concentrated on demonstrating the relationship linking the condition of the soul and the period of mourning to the state of the corpse during the period preceding the final burial; but we do not maintain that the three terms are indissolubly tied together and cannot be found in isolation. This absolute assertion would be immediately contradicted by the facts; indeed it is hardly necessary to say that a belief in a temporary stay of the soul on earth and the institution of prolonged mourning are found in societies where no double burial has been reported. The end of the period of waiting is sometimes set conventionally: thus among certain Indian tribes of South America a rope is tied to the corpse, which is buried at once, and its extremity remains visible on the surface of the tomb; when this rope has vanished, as a result of rain or wear, it is an indication that the soul of the deceased, which was near the corpse until then, has finally left for the other world.[148] But most often, when the deceased receives final burial without delay, it is the ideas relative to the passage of time itself which determine the end of the observances.[149] The death will not be fully consummated, the soul will not leave the earth, the mourning of the living will not be ended till a certain period of time, considered complete, has elapsed; this period may be a month or a year; the coming of that day will then mark the close of the bad phase, the beginning of another life. Often it is the belief in the eminence and sanctity of a particular number which influences the choice:

that is probably how we should explain the fact, so common among South American tribes, that the length of the soul's stay on earth or its journey to the other world is set at four days.[150] Should we look upon these facts as detached and modified parts of the more complex whole that we have analysed? It is seldom possible to answer this question with certainty, but one would be tempted to answer in the affirmative if our view were accepted that there is a natural connection between the beliefs concerning the disintegration of the body, the fate of the soul, and the state of the survivors during that same period.

2. THE FINAL CEREMONY

The custom of a great feast connected with the final burial is general among the Indonesians; it is to be found under different names in most islands of the Malay Archipelago, from the Nicobars on the west to Halmahera on the east. This feast, which lasts for several days, sometimes even a month,[151] is of extreme importance to the natives:[152] it requires elaborate preparations and expenses which often reduce the family of the deceased to extreme poverty;[153] many animals[154] are sacrificed and eaten in banquets that often degenerate into huge orgies; invitations for this occasion are sent out to all the surrounding villages and they are never refused.[155] In this way the feast tends to acquire a collective character; the expenses usually exceed the resources of a single family and, furthermore, such an interruption of normal life cannot be repeated often. Among the Olo Ngaju, the *tivah* is usually celebrated for several deceased persons at one time, the families concerned sharing the expenses.[156] In other societies the feast is repeated at regular intervals—every three years, for instance—and is celebrated in common for all those who have died in the meantime;[157] it thus no longer directly concerns the family of a particular dead person, but the village as a whole.

The final ceremony has three objects: to give burial to the remains of the deceased, to ensure the soul peace and access to the land of the dead, and finally to free the living from the obligations of mourning.

(a) The final burial

Among the Dayak of southeast Borneo, the final resting-place of the body is a small house, made entirely of iron-wood, often finely carved, and raised on fairly high posts of the same material; such a monument is called *sandong*, and constitutes a family burial place which can hold a large number of people,[158] and lasts many years. There are two kinds, which differ only in their contents and dimensions: the *sandong raung*, intended to hold coffins containing the dried remains of the deceased, and the *sandong tulang*, very much smaller, intended to hold only the bones wrapped in a cloth, or enclosed in an urn, and which have often been incinerated previously.[159] There is no fixed place for this monument: often it is erected in the immediate neighbour-hood of the house, inside the palisade which protects the village;[160] often too it is erected fairly far away, on land speci-ally reserved for the family.[161]

These two types of final burial place are not peculiar to the southeastern Dayak; they are found among other tribes in Borneo itself and on other islands.[162] We might perhaps be justified in relating these two types of burial to more primitive forms which are also found in the same ethnic family. The *sandong tulang* seems to be derived from a custom still in practice among the tribes of the interior of Borneo which consists in enclosing the remains of the de-ceased inside the trunk of an iron-wood tree which has been hollowed out for the purpose;[163] and the *sandong raung* is probably only a modification of the custom, very common in the Malay Archipelago, by which all the coffins containing the bones are finally laid together in crevices in rocks or in underground caves.[164]

These variations in the type of final burial place[165] are however of secondary importance to us; the important thing is that in most cases it has a collective, at the very least familial, character; in this it contrasts clearly with the temporary burial in which, as we have seen, the corpse is usually isolated. The transfer of the remains, at the time of the final ceremony, is therefore not a mere change of place; it brings about a profound change in the condition of the deceased; it delivers him from the isolation in which he was plunged since his death, and reunites his body with those of his ancestors.[166] This much emerges clearly from the study of the rites practised in the course of the second funeral.

The remains of the person or persons for whom the feast is to be celebrated are taken from their provisional sepulture and are brought back to the village, into the sumptuously decorated men's house, or into a house specially erected for the purpose;[167] there they are laid on a sort of catafalque.[168] But first an operation has to be performed which, according to one author, is the essential act of this feast:[169] the bones are washed carefully.[170] If, as sometimes happens, the bones are not completely bare, the flesh still clinging to them is detached.[171] They are then put into a new wrapping, which is often precious.[172] These rites are far from insignificant: by purifying the body,[173] by giving the deceased a new attire, the living mark the end of one period and the beginning of another; they abolish a sinister past and give the deceased a new and glorified body[174] with which to enter worthily the company of his ancestors.

But he does not depart without having been bid a solemn farewell and without the last days of his earthly existence being filled with pomp. As soon as the coffin is placed on the catafalque, among the Olo Ngaju, the widower or widow sits down very close to it and says to the deceased: 'You are with us for a while still, then you will go away to the pleasant place where our ancestors live. . .' They try to satisfy the deceased by displaying near his bones the sacred vases and most precious treasures belonging to the family, which he enjoyed during his life-time and which will assure him an opulent life in the other world.[175]

The Alfuru of Central Celebes dance round the remains of the dead during the month preceding the feast. Then, when the guests have arrived, priestesses take the wrapped-up bones in their arms and parade them inside the feast-house for two days, singing all the while: in this way, we are told, the living welcome the dead among them for the last time and show them the same affection as during their life, before they take final leave of their remains and their souls.[176]

If the burial place is distant and near the river (as is often the case with the Olo Ngaju) the body is laid in a brilliantly decorated boat, while the priestesses and relatives of the deceased take their places in another. When they arrive at the *sandong* and the bones are put into it, the priestesses perform a dance round the monument and 'beg the souls who are already buried there to welcome the newcomers'. Is this really a prayer? In fact, this dance and these songs, by their own virtue, give the material act just performed its meaning and its full efficacy: they permit the dead to enter the communion of his forefathers, in the same way as his bones have just been reunited with theirs in the *sandong*. The living now depart, with the feeling that they no longer owe their dead anything. Whereas they were silent when they came, to the sound of funeral music, they now return gaily, singing and drinking.[177] This contrast clearly marks the meaning of secondary funerals: they close the dark period dominated by death, and open a new era.

The feelings which the living experience towards the bones after these rites differ from those inspired by the corpse during the preceding period. Of course, the bones are still endowed with a character such that a too close contact with them seems dreadful and it is often preferred to put a fair distance between the house of the dead and the living;[178] but henceforth the element of repulsion and disgust is no longer dominant, but rather a feeling of reverent confidence. They believe that a beneficent influence emanates from the bones which protects the village against misfortune and helps the living in their enterprises.[179] It needs only a development and crystallisation of these beliefs and these feelings for a proper cult of relics to be established which causes a serious change in the nature of the final obsequies.

Indeed, especially when dealing with chiefs or important figures, the high esteem in which the virtues of their remains are held, and the desire to benefit from them, induce some tribes to give them a permanent place in the house of the living. In the Malay Archipelago it is almost always the head alone that enjoys this privilege;[180] it is the essential part of the body and the seat of the dead person's powers. After the head is decorated it is placed inside the house or in a small niche close to it; in certain cases it is offered food or is anointed with a special liquid: it is part of the family's sacred treasure and ensures its prosperity.[181] Thus the remains of the dead are not always finally reunited with their fathers in a common tomb; but this alteration of the rite does not seriously alter its meaning. The very existence of a reliquary cult presupposes the notion that there is no possibility of absolute continuity between the community of the living and that of the dead: by returning to take their place in the heart of the family, as venerated and protective ancestors, these distinguished dead re-enter communion with the family; but, too famous and too powerful to be lost among the hosts of the dead, they receive a place of honour near the living; and the cult of which they are from now on the object clearly indicates the change wrought in them by the final ceremony.

If favourable results are expected from the second obsequies, for the dead as well as for the living, the performance of this rite is nevertheless painful and feared because of the ultimate contact it entails with the very centre of the funereal infection.[182] Thus many tribes, as a result of either a spontaneous evolution or foreign influence, have come to spare themselves the bother and the risks of this ceremony. Some, for this reason, have advanced the celebration of the feast they owe to the deceased so as to make it coincide with the immediate funeral, which thus becomes the final one.[183] Elsewhere the feast has kept its date but only traces of the original custom of change of sepulture have survived. Thus the Alfuru of central Celebes who have become Muslim no longer exhume the corpse at the final ceremony; they limit themselves to pulling out all the weeds from the grave, to removing the small house that covers it and placing there new bark clothes[184] and provisions for the great journey that the soul has to make.[185] Were these survivals to fade, it would soon be forgotten that one of the essential objects of the final ceremony was to transfer the purified bones from the temporary resting-place to the final and collective sepulture.

(b) *The admittance of the soul to the land of the dead*

Parallel to that which is done to the remains of the deceased, a funeral service is performed which changes the condition of the soul: namely, it puts an end to its anxiety by solemnly introducing it into the society of the dead. It is an arduous task which requires powerful help, since the road that leads to the other world is strewn with perils of all kinds,[186] and the soul will not reach the end of the journey unless it is led and protected by some powerful psychopomp, such as Tempon Telon of the Olo Ngaju.[187] In order to guarantee this indispensable help to the soul, priests and priestesses, summoned by the family of the deceased, recite long incantations to the accompaniment of a drum.[188]

First they must go beyond the clouds to invite the celestial spirits to descend on earth where the souls await them:[189] docile, they arrive and at the request of the relatives they begin to load their boat; they put in to it not only the souls of the dead but also those of the animals which have been sacrificed for the feast and those of the treasures that have been displayed at it. To the sound of drums and the firing of guns the boat, steered by Tempon Telon, starts on its rapid course.[190] As the climax of the drama approaches, emotion becomes more intense; those present listen in silence, whilst the principal officiant is the prey of a true frenzy; his features are twisted, he foams at the mouth, and his body is bathed in sweat; he seems to identify himself with Tempon Telon (whose attributes, moreover, he bears); he sees the perils that threaten his boat and the whirlwind of fire which has to be passed through. At last a shout of triumph is heard that brings relief to the hearers:[191] they are saved, the town of the dead has been reached! . . . The souls alight, they begin to dance around their new home, they congratulate themselves: 'The day of our victory has come. Here we are, led by Tempon Telon, far from the earthly shore where the spears of men gather; we can see the rich town where gold glitters.' Then, after eating the generous meal provided for them at the feast, they summon their slaves[192] who adorn them, oil their hair and blacken their teeth; and their hearts rejoice! Then the ancestors, who have lived so long in the land of the dead, gather and come to welcome the new arrivals.[193] However, the latter are not yet completely re-established. A new journey (and a special song)[194] are necessary so that the souls of the bones, the hair and the nails, awakened from their long stupor, shall also arrive in the heavenly city and rejoin their master. The task is now completed. The shade is embodied once more, the exiled and wandering soul now has a fixed place among its own kind;[195] an opulent existence,[196] that seems to perpetuate indefinitely the splendours and extreme abundance of the funeral feast itself, succeeds the precarious life that the soul has led on earth since death. In short, after this last trial the soul is freed, it is saved.[197]

If we are to believe the missionary Braches, this description of the soul's journey and of the heavenly village is but a fable unscrupulously invented by the priestly psychopomps; actually, for the latter, as for all the Dayak, the soul is tied to the bodily remains and lives inside or near the *sandong*.[198] There is in fact a close tie between the container of the bones and the 'town of the dead': it is the soul or spiritual substance of the charnel-house, and of the brilliant accessories around it, which after undergoing a transformation will form in the sky the home and the treasures of the deceased.[199] The magical songs merely translate into the language of myth the rites performed over the bones. But this translation is not a lying fiction. Undoubtedly 'the single consolation of the Dayak lies in the thought that one day he will be reunited with his ancestors';[200] but this reunion, which as far as the deceased is concerned is the main object of the final ceremony, is achieved by two different acts; by the placing of the remains in a communal tomb and by the admittance of the soul to the collective abode of the dead. These two events are conjoined and equally essential: the rite provides material support for the conception; the imagination prolongs and completes what is merely outlined by the rite.

The soul does not enter the celestial city in order to enjoy an eternal rest there: immortality no more belongs to the inhabitants of the other world than it does to those of this. The soul stays in heaven for a period of seven generations, but each time it has reached the end of one existence it must die in order to be reborn.[201] After its seventh death, the soul descends on earth again and enters a mushroom or a fruit, preferably near the village. When a woman eats this fruit or mushroom, the soul enters her body and is soon reborn in human form. But if the fruit is eaten by certain animals, a buffalo, a deer or a monkey, the soul will be reincarnated in an animal body; should this animal be eaten by man, the soul will return among humanity by this detour.[202] If on the other hand the fruit or the animal dies without having been eaten, the soul then fades away for ever.[203] Except for this case, which among the Olo Ngaju seems exceptional, we see that the soul is destined to pass incessantly through the cycle of deaths and rebirths, and that its stay in heaven among the ancestors is only a stage separating two incarnations, whether human or animal, on earth. Death, for these people, is therefore not a singular event occurring only once in the history of an individual: it is an episode that repeats itself endlessly and that merely marks the passage from one form of existence to another.

By putting an end to the troubles of the soul, the final ceremony removes every cause that the soul has had since its death to be ill-disposed towards the living. It is still true, of course, that even after the great funeral feast the dead belong to another world, and that a too intimate contact with them is dangerous for the living.[204] However, the souls generally leave their relatives alone once the latter have discharged their last duties towards them.[205] In many cases, this negative position is not all: there are regular relations and an exchange of services between the community of the living and that of the dead.[206] In certain Indonesian societies the appeased souls are actually worshipped, and they then settle near the domestic hearth in some consecrated object or in a statuette of the deceased which they animate: their presence, duly honoured, guarantees the prosperity of the living.[207] Thus the act that re-unites the soul of the deceased to those of his ancestors sometimes confers on it the character of a tutelary divinity, and solemnly ensures its return to the heart of the family home.[208]

(c) The liberation of the living

The customs examined so far have dealt with the welfare of the deceased; any benefit to the living was merely incidental. But we find a series of no less important practices performed at the funeral feast, whose direct object is to end the mourning of the relatives of the deceased and to bring these back into communion with society.[209]

On the first day of the *tivah*, after a banquet attended only by women, one of these prepares seven small parcels of rice for the souls of the dead, and seven others for the evil spirits; at the same time she pronounces a formula which clearly reveals the meaning of this act: 'I place here your food; by this I crush all resistance, all that is impure, all bad dreams, and I set an end to all tears.'[210] This offering is the signal that the time has come for the living to part from the dead and to dispel the unease which has enveloped them during the mourning. It is only the first manifestation of a theme which will be taken up many times during the feast.

The living, especially the relatives of the deceased, occupy the central place in the song of the priestesses which leads the souls into the celestial city. During the entire time of the incantations, the priestesses carry the souls of the givers of the feast in their aprons, like small children;[211] each time they ascend to heaven to ask the good spirits for help, they take their protégés with them. Also a kind of fascination draws the souls of the living towards the regions above: they have to be recalled by name if they are not to stay in the other world where they have followed the dead.[212] But these spiritual journeys are not made in vain. The priestesses never fail to call the spirits' attention to the givers of the feast: 'Rise', they call to the most powerful among the spirits, 'squeeze the body[213] of this man here to drive misfortune from him, remove the stench that petrifies like the thunderbolt, dispel the impure cloud of the deceased, repel the fate that degrades and that causes life to retreat. . . .'[214] It is not enough to 'kill the adversity'[215] which oppressed the living. Tempon Telon must regenerate[216] them and ensure their long life by sprinkling their body with revivifying water. He has also to give them 'the potent charms which secure wealth, success in commerce, and the lustre of glory'.[217] Naturally, the priestesses simultaneously perform the acts which their song imposes on, or ascribes to, the celestial spirits;[218] and these rites, both oral and manual, bring about a profound change in the living:[219] delivered from the evil which possessed them, they return to normal life with a new fund of vital and social power.[220]

But if the living are to be rid of their impurity a sacrifice is essential, preferably that which in the eyes of the Dayak and most Indonesians has irresistable efficacy: the sacrifice of a human victim whose head is cut off and afterwards kept.[221] An entire day, at the time of the *tivah*, is devoted to this essential rite. The prisoners or slaves, who have previously been deprived of their souls by a magical intervention, are chained to the sacrificial post; the male relatives of the deceased act collectively as sacrificers, dancing and leaping around the victim and striking him at random with their spears. The screams of pain are greeted with joyful shouts, because the more cruel the torture the happier the souls are in heaven. At last, when the victim falls to the ground he is solemnly decapitated in the midst of an intense joy; his blood is collected by a priestess who sprinkles it on the living 'to reconcile them with their deceased relative'; the head is either deposited with the bones of the deceased or attached to the top of a post erected near the *sandong*.[222] The funeral sacrifice, without any doubt, is not meant simply to release the family of the deceased from the taboo; its functions are as complex as the aim of the feast of which it is the decisive act. The mystic fury of the sacrificers, while it desacralises the living, gives peace and beatitude to the soul of the deceased and (probably) regenerates his his body.[223] The liberation of the mourners is only the most obvious among the changes brought about simultaneously by virtue of the sacrifice, that which interests the living most directly.[224]

Every religious ceremony must be followed by practices which free the participants from the dangerous character they have acquired and which enable them to re-enter the profane world. The rites acquire a special importance at the time of the funeral feast, to the extent sometimes of constituting a second feast, distinct from the first one and succeeding it. The perils incurred during a ceremony like the *tivah* are in fact particularly intense. No doubt it has beneficial consequences and constitutes a kind of victory over misfortune; but on the other hand it touches the kingdom of death and compels the living to enter into relations with the forces of evil and with the residents of the other world. That is why the relatives of the deceased and also those who have taken part in the funeral proceedings are compelled to purify themselves. They bathe in the river, and to increase the effectiveness of this the blood of sacrificed animals is sometimes mixed with the water, and while they swim to the bank the priestesses, who follow them in boats, thrust aside evil influences from their bodies with the help of burning torches and sacred brooms.[225] At last, if all the rites have been correctly observed, the living are washed clean of all pollution and freed of the deathly contagion.

However, those who were excluded from the society by their mourning do not have to wait till these last practices are carried out in order to be solemnly reintegrated into it. Their clothes are changed for new ones fixed by custom; they make their toilet; the men fasten on their fine swords and the women resume their ornaments. A great banquet, to which the guests contribute their part, and gay dances mark the raising of the ban which weighed upon the near relatives of the deceased: they are now free to mix with other people and to resume ordinary life.[226] It can be seen that there is a complete parallelism between the rites which introduce the deceased, washed and dressed in new clothes, into the company of his ancestors, and those which return his family to the community of the living: or rather it is one and the same act of liberation applied to two different categories of persons.

The societies dealt with in the preceding study belong to a relatively advanced type of civilisation: totemism is scarcely to be found in it, and then only in traces here and there. Yet a religious system which so deeply affects the organisation and the life of societies where it is dominant must obviously set its mark on the beliefs relative to death and the other world, and consequently on the funeral ritual. It is thus particularly interesting to us to determine the nature of the final burial in a society where totemism exists as a living institution. The observations of Spencer and Gillen on the tribes of central Australia give us the necessary elements of information.

Let us recall briefly the beliefs on which the totemic organisation of these tribes rests. Each totemic group now in existence traces its origin to one or several ancestors,[227] half-human, half-animal, who emerged from the earth in very remote times. These ancestors roamed the tribal territory in all directions, stopping in certain places to make camps and to hold sacred ceremonies; finally they sank back into the ground. But they did not disappear altogether, because in each place where they had lived and where some of them had died[228] they left behind their souls as well as certain other souls they were carrying with them. In this way they founded a multitude of spirit colonies, each connected to some particular natural object such as a tree or a rock. It is these souls which, by their successive rebirths, constitute the human totemic group as well as the eponymous species;[229] for each living member of the tribe is merely the temporary reincarnation either of a particular ancestor whose name he bears in certain cases,[230] or of one of the souls which have issued from him.[231]

Among the Binbinga, about a year after death,[232] a messenger sent by the father of the deceased goes out to summon other groups of the tribe; he carries with him a bone from the arm of the deceased, painted red and wrapped in a ritual manner. This sacred object makes his

E

person inviolable and no one to whom it has been presented can refrain from following him. Once the strangers have arrived and relations have been established, by appropriate rites, between them and their hosts, the real ceremony begins: in the evening and all through the following night they chant sacred songs connected with the totemic ancestor of the deceased. The next day, the individuals belonging to the group of which the deceased was a member adorn themselves with the symbol of their totem and execute the rythmic movements accompanied by songs which constitute most of the totemic ceremonies. Finally the bones, which have been brought to the consecrated ground on the previous day by the father, are placed in a hollowed trunk on the outside of which have been painted representations of the deceased's totem. This coffin is put in the branches of a tree overhanging a pond and is not touched from then on; the place is sacred, at least for a time, and women may not come near it.[233]

The final ceremony of the Warramunga[234] differs from the above in some important points. Firstly, the essential rites are not performed over all of the bones,[235] but over one bone from the arm which has been set apart and carefully wrapped: here we have a phenomenon of the substitution of the part for the whole which is commonly found; and the choice of the radius bone is probably to be explained by the close connection which is thought to exist between it and the soul of the individual.[236] Moreover, the last funeral rite always takes place immediately after the end of a series of ceremonies connected with the ancestor of the totemic group to which the deceased belonged, or at least a group of the same phratry.[237] In one of the cases cited by Spencer and Gillen the final burial was to be given to a woman whose totem was the great mythical snake Wollunqua. Seventeen days earlier the radius of the dead woman had been solemnly brought back to the camp and entrusted to the care of the women charged with watching and crying over it:

the end was awaited of the long sacred drama which reproduces and repeats the chief actions of the ancestor from the time of his emergence from the earth to his final disappearance.[238] As soon as this last act was completed the women brought the radius, still wrapped, to the place of the ceremony. Suddenly it was torn from them;[239] with one swing of an axe a man smashed it to pieces,[240] and then laid the fragments in a small grave. This he had dug himself near a drawing traced in the earth showing the serpent disappearing underground, leaving behind it the souls of its descendants.[241] The grave was then closed with a flat stone. This rite shows that 'the time of mourning is over and the deceased has been reunited with his totem'. A significant detail is that in the Warramunga language one and the same word designates the final burial of the radius, the totemic drawing, and the action by which the various ancestors went underground.[242] So each individual returns finally to the bosom of his totem, and his death merges with the death of the ancestor whose reincarnation he is.

Death, which is consummated by the final ceremony, is not an annihilation; as the ancestor has left his soul behind, so also will the descendant in whom this soul has lived for a while. This belief is found not only in the above mentioned tribes but also among the Arunta, who bury the corpse immediately after death.[243] At the end of an intermediary period, during which the soul haunts the burial place or the camp of the living,[244] it goes to meet the other souls of its totem at the very place where it used to live in the days of the ancestors and where it resided between incarnations.[245] Naturally, we have only rather vague reports about the condition of the disembodied soul and its mode of existence. However, we are told that in the eyes of the Australian aborigine such a spirit is a very real personage whose image merges with that of the ancestors who gave birth to the totemic groups. Like them, he possesses far greater powers than the present and living members of the tribe.[246]

Although it is true that he generally uses these powers to perform good deeds, care must be taken not to offend him by ex-
cessive familiarity. Like the ancestors, the spirits roam over the
countryside, but only at night, camping in certain places and
performing their ceremonies which, according to the Arunta,
they sometimes reveal to certain privileged individuals.[247]

Since some of the ancestors were in the form of the animal whose name they bore,[248] one might expect to see the
soul, after death, join the appropriate body in the sacred
species. Strangely enough, the belief that death is a transformation of an individual into the animal of his totem is
not reported among the Australian tribes.[249] But it is found
in other societies, to such an extent that some authors have
seen in this belief the very basis of totemism;[250] and it is
sometimes manifested in the nature of the last funeral
rites. Thus among the Bororo, for example, each individual
is believed to become a specific animal after death, usually
a certain type of parakeet. One of the essential acts of the
final ceremony consists in the ritual decoration of the dry
bones: in the midst of sacred dances and songs, the bones are
entirely covered with the feathers of this parakeet.[251] The
meaning of the ceremony associated with the final burial
appears clearly here: the point is to give the deceased a new
body for the new life that he enters.

The Australian aborigines do not consider the return of
the soul to its primal condition as final: one day it will enter
the body of a woman, soon to recommence a human life.[252]
The period that elapses between death and rebirth is indefinite; it seems to depend entirely on the whim of the soul
and on the opportunities presented to it.[253] However, the
existence of a minimal interval is reported from two very
distinct tribes: according to the Arunta, the reincarnation
cannot take place before the bones themselves have turned
into dust; according to the Gnanji, it occurs when rain has
washed the bones and purified them.[254] Of course, too much
importance should not be attached to these particular

beliefs, which moreover are not very coherent; but a connection does seem to exist between the state of the bones and that of the soul. The latter cannot take its place again among men until the whole of the present body has disappeared. In any case, whenever it takes place, reincarnation is normal and anticipated. The rite by which the death of the individual is identified with the death of the ancestor results, at least indirectly, in preserving the souls which belong to the totemic group and in ensuring consequently the perpetuation and integrity of this group.

If we compare the final ceremony as it is found among central Australians with the Indonesian funeral feast, we cannot but be struck by the similarity that exists between these two forms of one and the same institution. Not only is it always a matter of bringing to an end the mourning of the close relatives,[255] but the end pursued is identical as far as the deceased himself is concerned. Like the Dayak, the Warramunga intend by means of the last funeral rite to complete the separation of the deceased from the living, and to ensure his entry into the community of the sacred ancestors. Like the Dayak, the Warramunga do not look upon this new existence as eternal: the liberation of the soul makes possible, and prepares for, a later return of the individual to the group he has just left. Beside this important concordance, we must note certain differences: the thought of reincarnation seems stronger and closer among the Australians than among the Indonesians. Consequently, among the former, the society of the dead has perhaps less stability and autonomy: instead of gathering in a common village, the souls are scattered over the surface of the tribal territory in a number of specified centres;[256] finally, and correlatively, we have not found a collective burial of bones among these tribes.[257] The reunion of the dead with their ancestors occurs here only in a mystical fashion, which can perhaps be explained by the vague character of the Australian totemic group.[258] Although the reunion of the deceased's bones with those of his ancestors does not exist in the central Australian tribes, it generally constitutes nevertheless one of the most important acts of the final ceremony. The ossuaries, whose existence is attested by numerous ethnologists, belong to the family or to the clan.[259] 'In life one house, in death one grave,' says a Malagasy proverb, expressing a widespread and deep feeling.[260] The Choctaw consider the mixing of a relative's bones with those of strangers criminal and sacrilegious, because those who are of one flesh and one bone must be reunited.[261] That is why so many peoples believe that the greatest calamity that can befall an individual is to die far away and thus to be separated from his kin for ever. The greatest efforts are made to bring his bones back to his native land and to join them to those of his fathers.[262] It seems that the group would consider itself diminished if it were to admit that one of its members could be permanently cut off from it.

The rite of reunion of the bones is elucidated, as Brinton has shown,[263] if it is compared with the practice, very common in America, of collecting the bones of animals killed in the hunt: the motive of this custom, sometimes explicit, is that 'the bones contain the souls of the animals and one day they will put on their flesh again and will repopulate the prairies'. Human bones are the object of the same belief; they contain the germ of a future existence,[264] and must therefore be treasured as security for the continued existence of the group. The ossuary of the clan is not only the communal residence where the ancestors meet, but also a reservoir of souls from which descendants will issue.

But collective ossuaries are not all familial, and the second funeral sometimes has an importance that goes far beyond the limits of the domestic group. The Ataruipe Cave, in the headwaters of the Orinoco, of which Alexander von Humboldt has given us a celebrated description, contained about six hundred skeletons, enclosed in baskets or in earthenware urns; it was 'the grave of an entire vanished people'.[265] Similarly, a great number of barrows and 'bone-ditches' found in various parts of the United States seem, by their size, to have been used as final burial places for large communities;[266] and this conjecture is confirmed by historical evidence.

Similarly, each of the four nations constituting the Confederation of Hurons observed the custom of periodically collecting the remains of their dead in a communal grave. This ceremony, held every ten or twelve years and called the 'Feast of the Souls', was, we are told, 'the most brilliant and solemn of all observances among these savages'. Each family, at the proper time, would exhume the remains of those relatives who had died since the last feast; the bones were cleaned of such flesh as might still be adhering to them,[267] dressed in new clothes and adorned with bead necklaces or with garlands. Then, after a domestic ceremony,[268] everyone was ready to start for the central meeting place, which was often very distant. This funeral procession was not without perils; for the dried bones, which were called souls, were a terrible burden that could give the bearers a pain in the side for life if they did not often take the precaution of 'imitating the cry of the souls', which eased their lot greatly. The final rite was celebrated in the midst of an enormous crowd. The chiefs, in the name of the dead, made a general distribution of presents, which went largely to strangers invited to the feast since it was held important that they should admire the country's magnificence.[269] We find here, in a striking form, a phenomenon already observed among the Indonesians: the final ceremony always has a pronounced collective character and entails a concentration of the society. But here it is not the family or even the village, but the nation, that intervenes directly to reintegrate the dead into social communion.[270] This action thus takes on a political significance:[271] by dealing with all their dead in common the various domestic and local groups that form the higher unity become conscious of, and

consequently maintain, the ties that unite them. In establishing
a society of the dead, the society of the living regularly recreates itself.

However, secondary reasons may modify the nature of
the second burial. The bones of the dead are usually sacred
and magically potent; they are 'warm with spiritual
power'.[272] There is therefore reason to fear that enemies
might desecrate the familial tomb and the energies lying
in the bones, in order to serve their own hostile designs;
such a profanation is the worst of calamities for the family.[273]
On the other hand, one can hope that by keeping the bones
close by one will have a precious reserve of beneficial forces.
This fear and this hope are the reason why the final burial
sometimes consists in bringing the bones back to the family's
house[274] or in distributing them among the relatives of
the deceased, who will wear them. Thus in the Andaman
Islands it is rare to see an adult person who does not wear
at least a necklace of human bones; this is not a mere ornament but a defence against the attacks of evil spirits.[275]
The contact is sometimes even more intimate; for various
South American tribes cremate and pulverise the bones at
the final ceremony in order to rub their body with the pow-
der or swallow it with their drink. The explanation given
by some Indians is interesting: since they believe that the
soul resides in the bones, they hope that by eating them
they will resurrect the deceased inside themselves.[276]

As in Indonesia, the second burial is very often a ceremony intended to give the soul peace and beatitude.
There is a close link between the soul and the bones;[277]
and the rites which purify, adorn, and strengthen them,
and finally lead them to a consecrated spot, all have their
effect upon the soul's condition. Furthermore, special
incantations and dramatic rites aim directly at releasing
the soul from the grasp of death.

The ceremony performed to this effect by the Mabuiag
Islanders is particularly instructive: during the period

following its arrival in the land of the dead, the soul remains a kind of unstable shadow. The soul of a friend, previously deceased, welcomes it and conceals it. Then, on the first night of the new moon, it is introduced by the same friend to the company of souls; these strike the new soul on the head with a mass of stones. The newcomer then becomes a true spirit and is instructed in all the secrets of the other world. During this transformation, which is naturally performed on earth by people disguised as spirits, the relatives and friends of the deceased lament, because they say 'they are initiating him, he is now a true spirit and will forget us all'.[278] It is at that time that the separation between the deceased and this world becomes final. It is so true that natural death is not sufficient to sever the ties binding the deceased to this world, that in order to become a legitimate and authentic inhabitant of the land of the dead he must first be killed. Even though the word itself is not pronounced, we have here a true initiation and, in the same way as the secrets of the group are not revealed to a youth until he has passed the imposed tests, so the deceased cannot pass from his miserable state to one of happiness, cannot be promoted to the ranks of the true spirits, until he has been ritually killed and has been born anew. We can thus understand why the great journey of the soul is usually regarded as difficult and perilous, why the priests or medicine-men charged with conducting the soul have to put forth all their strength to reach the desired end, and why, finally, the onlookers await the outcome with anxiety. Not that the group can really doubt the final deliverance; in its eyes the rite, so long as it is correctly performed, has an irresistible efficacy. But these very anxieties and arduous efforts are necessary, just as there could be no initiation without pain being inflicted and borne. The imaginary trials encountered by the soul on its way to heaven constitute a true sacrament whose effect is to regenerate the deceased and to give him entry to the other world.

The final ceremony thus profoundly alters the condition
of the deceased: it awakens him from his bad sleep[279] and
enables him to live a secure social life again. It makes a
wandering shade into a 'Father'.[280] This transformation
does not differ essentially from a true resurrection. In the
myths and fables, where the collective imagination has free
rein, the two phenomena are often even fused: a breath or an
invigorating aspersion are enough to give the bones flesh
and spirit again;[281] the dead rise again and take up the
thread of their interrupted life. But in real life one just has
to accept irrevocable fact. However strong their desire,
men dare not hope for themselves 'a death like that of the
moon or the sun, which plunge into the darkness of Hades,
to rise again in the morning, endowed with new strength'.[282]
The funeral rites cannot entirely nullify the work of death:
those who have been struck by it will return to life, but it
will be in another world or as other species.

The soul does not always have to stay a time in the land of
the ancestral spirits before being able to re-enter the body of
a child. Sometimes the reincarnation takes place immediately
after the end of the funeral period;[283] and often one of the
souls, the one that is directly connected with the body, can
migrate into the womb of a woman without any set delay
and return to earth; the date of this supposed transmigration
seems to depend solely upon the birth of a child in the family
of the deceased.[284] This is shown by the rule observed by
various peoples for the transmission of the name,[285] by the
Eskimos in particular. When a child is born it is given the
name of the last person in the village who died or of a relative who died far away. The effect of this ceremony is to
transfer the name, which up till then has remained in the
proximity of the new-born child. This, says one author, is
called 'the reanimation or resurrection of the deceased'
and ensures the peace of his soul. At the same time it relieves
the relatives of their mourning, who see the one they have
lost return in a new form. The child in fact is the living

incarnation of the individual whose name he bears; he is supposed to inherit his talents and will represent him at feasts for the dead.[286] The name of the deceased must never be uttered until he has started his new life.[287] This prohibition is also found among the Chinook, but it ends with the final funeral.[288] In fact, the application of the deceased's name to a new-born child is, in a sense, equivalent to the final ceremony: like the latter, it pacifies the deceased and returns him to life, putting an end to the funeral peril and taboo.[289]

We have seen that in Indonesia the feast that ends the funeral rites simultaneously releases the living from the obligation to mourn; this is a constant feature. The content of the rite may vary but the general meaning of it is fixed: the relatives of the deceased are unburdened of the dangerous character that misfortune has bestowed upon them, and they receive a 'new body',[290] such as normal life demands; they part finally with death and with evil forces,[291] in order to make their rightful re-entry into the world of the living.[292]

The institution of secondary burial, whose meaning and generality we have tried to show, often undergoes a marked regression.[293] In some societies unmistakable traces of the original custom subsist: the Dene, for instance, at a certain time after death open the sarcophagus holding the remains of the deceased and merely look at them without daring to run the risk and pollution entailed by contact with the corpse. After a meal has been offered to the souls the tomb is closed for ever.[294] Among other peoples, the last rite consists in trampling on the grave,[295] or in sealing it by the erection of a funeral monument.[296] Only then does the deceased come into full possession of the place which up till that time he merely occupied. In other cases, even these survivals are not found: the only object of the feast is to terminate the funeral period,[297] to put an end to the period of mourning, or to make final provision for the well-being of the disembodied soul. But these functions in turn are removed from the final ceremony or lose their importance. We have seen that there is a close solidarity between the body and the soul of the deceased: if the true funeral takes place immediately after death, one tends naturally to ensure the salvation of the soul from that moment on. On the other hand, the mourning has changed in nature; it is no longer a question of the survivors marking their participation in the present condition of the deceased, but of expressing a sorrow that is considered obligatory. Hence the duration of the mourning is no longer dependent on ideas about the deceased: it is entirely determined by causes of a domestic or social kind. Furthermore, special practices are no longer needed to liberate the relatives of the deceased; they regain their former position unaided at the end of the prescribed period. Thus impoverished, the final ceremony is now merely a simple anniversary service, whose only object is to pay last respects to the deceased and to commemorate his death.

3. Conclusion

It is impossible to interpret the body of facts that we have presented if we see in death a merely physical event. The horror inspired by the corpse does not spring from the simple observation of the changes that occur in the body. Proof that such a simplistic explanation is inadequate lies in the fact that in one and the same society the emotion aroused by death varies extremely in intensity according to the social status of the deceased, and may even in certain cases be entirely lacking. At the death of a chief, or of a man of high rank, a true panic sweeps over the group; the corpse is so powerfully contagious that among the Kaffir the entire kraal must be deserted at once and even enemies would not be willing to live there.[298] On the contrary, the death of a stranger, a slave, or a child[299] will go almost unnoticed; it will arouse no emotion, occasion no ritual.[300] It is thus not as the extinction of an animal life that death occasions social beliefs, sentiments and rites.

Death does not confine itself to ending the visible bodily life of an individual; it also destroys the social being grafted upon the physical individual and to whom the collective consciousness attributed great dignity and importance. The society of which that individual was a member formed him by means of true rites of consecration, and has put to work energies proportionate to the social status of the deceased: his destruction is tantamount to a sacrilege,[301] implying the intervention of powers of the same order but of a negative nature. God's handiwork can be undone only by himself or by Satan.[302] This is why primitive peoples do not see death as a natural phenomenon: it is always due to the action of spiritual powers, either because the deceased has brought disaster upon himself by violating some taboo, or because an enemy has 'killed' him by means of spells or magical practices.[303] The ethnographers who report this widespread belief see in it a gross and persistent error; but we ought rather to consider it as the naïve expression of a permanent social need. Indeed society imparts its own character of permanence to the individuals who compose it: because it feels itself immortal and wants to be so, it cannot normally believe that its members, above all those in whom it incarnates itself and with whom it identifies itself, should be fated to die. Their destruction can only be the consequence of a sinister plot. Of course, reality brutally contradicts this assumption, but the denial is always received with the same indignant amazement and despair. Such an attack must have an author upon whom the group may vent its anger. Sometimes the deceased himself is accused: 'What cause did you have, you ingrate, to forsake us?' And he is summoned to return. More often the near relatives are accused of culpable negligence[304] or of witchcraft; the sorcerers must at all costs be discovered and executed; or, finally, curses are directed against the murderous spirits, as by the Naga, for instance, who threaten them with their spears and defy them to appear.[305]

Thus, when a man dies, society loses in him much more than a unit; it is stricken in the very principle of its life, in the faith it has in itself. Consider the accounts by ethnographers of the scenes of furious despair which take place when death sets in or immediately after the expiry. Among the Warramunga, for instance, men and women throw themselves pell-mell on the dying person, in a compact mass, screaming and mutilating themselves atrociously.[306] It seems that the entire community feels itself lost, or at least directly threatened by the presence of antagonistic forces: the very basis of its existence is shaken.[307] As for the deceased, both victim and prisoner of evil powers, he is violently ejected from the society, dragging his closest relatives with him.

But this exclusion is not final. In the same way as the collective consciousness does not believe in the necessity of death, so it refuses to consider it irrevocable. Because it believes in itself a healthy society cannot admit that an individual who was part of its own substance,[308] and on whom it has set its mark, shall be lost for ever. The last word must remain with life: the deceased will rise from the grip of death and will return, in one form or another, to the peace of human association. This release and this reintegration constitute, as we have seen, one of the most solemn actions of collective life in the least advanced societies we can find. And when, closer to us, the Christian Church guarantees 'the resurrection and the life'[309] to all those who have fully entered it, it only expresses, in a rejuvenated form, the promise that every religious society implicitly makes to its members.

Only what was elsewhere the achievement of the group itself, acting through special rites, here becomes the attribute of a divine being, of a Saviour who by his sacrificial death has triumphed over death and freed his disciples from it; resurrection, instead of being the consequence of a particular ceremony, is a consequence, postponed for an indeterminate period, of God's grace.[310] Thus, at whatever stage of religious evolution we place ourselves, the notion of death is linked with that of resurrection; exclusion is always followed by a new integration.

Once the individual has surmounted death, he will not simply return to the life he has left; the separation has been too serious to be abolished so soon. He is reunited with those who, like himself and those before him, have left this world and gone to the ancestors. He enters this mythical society of souls which each society constructs in its own image. But the heavenly or subterranean city is not a mere replica of the earthly city. By recreating itself beyond death, society frees itself from external constraints and physical necessities which, here on earth, constantly hinder the flight of the collective desire. Precisely because the other world exists only in the mind, it is free of all limitations: it is—or can be[311]—the realm of the ideal. There is no longer any reason why game should not be perpetually abundant in the 'happy hunting-grounds' of the other world, or why every day of the eternal life should not be a Sunday to the Englishman eager for psalms. Moreover, in some societies, the way in which earthly life ends is a kind of blemish; death spreads its shadow over this world, and the very victory that the soul has gained over death opens up for it an infinitely pure and more beautiful life.[312] These notions, of course, do not appear at first in a clear-cut and precise form. It is especially when the religious society is differentiated from domestic or political social life that death seems to free the believer from the bodily and temporal calamities which kept him separated from God while on earth. Death enables him, regenerated, to enter the community of Saints, the invisible church which in heaven is worthy of being about the Lord from whom it proceeds. But the same conception is present, in a vague and concealed form, from the beginning of religious evolution: in rejoining his forefathers, the deceased is reborn transfigured and raised to a superior power and dignity. In other words, in the eyes of primitives, death is an initiation.[313]

This statement is not a mere metaphor; if death, for the collective consciousness, is indeed the passage from the visible society to the invisible, it is also a step exactly analogous to that by which a youth is withdrawn from the company of women and introduced into that of adult men. This new integration, which gives the individual access to the sacred mysteries of the tribe, also implies a profound change in his personality, a renewal of his body and soul that gives him the religious and moral capacity he needs. The similarity of the two phenomena is so fundamental that this change is often brought about by the pretended death of the aspirant, followed by his resurrection into a superior life.[314]

Death, as it is seen by the collective consciousness, should not be compared only with initiation. The close relationship that exists between funeral rites and rites of birth or marriage has often been noticed.[315] Like death, these two events give rise to an important ceremony in which a certain anxiety is mixed with the joy. In all three cases, the mystical dangers incurred must be guarded against, and purificatory rites must be observed. The similarity of these practices expresses a basic analogy: marriage brings about a double change of status; on the one hand it withdraws the fiancée from her own clan or family in order to introduce her into the clan or family of the husband; and on the other hand, it transfers her from the class of young girls into that of married women. As for birth, it accomplishes, for the collective consciousness, the same transformation as death but the other way round. The individual leaves the invisible and mysterious world that his soul has inhabited, and he enters the society of the living. This transition from one group to another, whether real or imaginary, always supposes a profound renewal of the individual which is marked by such customs as the acquisition of a new name, the changing of clothes or of the way of life. This operation is considered to be full of risks because it involves a stirring to action of necessary but dangerous forces. The body of the new-born child is no less sacred than the corpse.[316] The veil of the bride and that of the widow are of different colours, but they nonetheless have the same function, which is to isolate and set apart a redoubtable person.[317]

Thus death is not originally conceived as a unique event without any analogue. In our civilisation, the life of an individual seems to go on in approximately the same way from birth to death; the successive stages of our social life are weakly marked and constantly allow the continuous thread of the individual life to be discerned. But less advanced societies, whose internal structure is clumsy and rigid, conceive the life of a man as a succession of heterogeneous and well-defined phases, to each of which corresponds a more or less organised social class.[318] Consequently, each promotion of the individual implies the passage from one group to another: an exclusion, i.e. a death, and a new integration, i.e. a rebirth. Of course these two elements do not always appear on the same level: according to the nature of the change produced, it is sometimes the one and sometimes the other on which the collective attention is focused, and which determines the dominant character of the event; but both elements are in fact complementary. To the social consciousness, death is only a particular instance of a general phenomenon.

It is easy for us to understand now why death has long been looked upon as a transitory state of a certain duration. Every change of status in the individual, as he passes from one group to another, implies a deep change in society's mental attitude toward him, a change that is made gradually and requires time. The brute fact of physical death is not enough to consummate death in people's minds: the image of the recently deceased is still part of the system of things of this world, and looses itself from them only gradually by a series of internal partings. We cannot bring ourselves

F

to consider the deceased as dead straight away: he is too much part of our substance, we have put too much of ourselves into him, and participation in the same social life creates ties which are not to be severed in one day. The 'factual evidence' is assailed by a contrary flood of memories and images, of desires and hopes.[319] The evidence imposes itself only gradually and it is not until the end of this prolonged conflict that we give in and believe in the separation as something real. This painful psychological process expresses itself in the objective and mystical shape of the belief that the soul only gradually severs the ties binding it to this world: it finds a stable existence again only when the representation of the deceased has acquired a final and pacified character in the consciousness of the survivors. There is too deep an opposition between the persisting image of a familiar person who is like ourselves and the image of an ancestor, who is sometimes worshipped and always distant,[320] for this second image to replace the former immediately. That is why the idea of an 'intermediary state between death and resurrection'[321] imposes itself, a state in which the soul is thought to free itself from the impurity of death or from the sin attaching to it.[322] Thus, if a certain period is necessary to banish the deceased from the land of the living, it is because society, disturbed by the shock, must gradually regain its balance;[323] and because the double mental process of disintegration and of synthesis that the integration of an individual into a new world supposes, is accomplished in a molecular fashion, as it were, which requires time.[324]

It seems that society cannot for long become conscious of itself and of the phenomena which constitute its life except in an indirect way, after it has been in a sense reflected in the material world. The infection which for a time takes possession of the body, shows in a perceptible form the temporary presence of evil spirits.[325] The gradual destruction of the earthly body, which prolongs and completes the initial assault, expresses concretely the state of bewilderment and anguish of the community for so long as the exclusion of the deceased has not been completed. On the other hand, the reduction of the corpse to bones, which are more or less unchangeable and upon which death will have no further hold, seems to be the condition and the sign of the final deliverance. Now that the body is similar to those of its ancestors, there seems to be no longer any obstacle to the soul's entering their community. It has often been remarked,[326] and rightly, that there is a close relationship between the representation of the body and that of the soul. This mental connection is necessary, not only because collective thought is primarily concrete and incapable of conceiving a purely spiritual existence, but above all because it has a profoundly stimulating and dramatic character. The group requires actions that will focus the attention of its members, orientate their imagination in a definite direction, and which will inspire the belief in everybody. The material on which the collective activity will act after the death, and which will be the object of the rites, is naturally the very body of the deceased. The integration of the deceased into the invisible society will not be effected unless his material remains are reunited with those of his forefathers. It is the action of society on the body that gives full reality to the imagined drama of the soul.[327] Thus, if the physical phenomena which constitute or follow death do not in themselves determine the collective representations and emotions, they nevertheless help to give them the particular form that they present, and lend them a degree of material support. Society projects its own ways of thinking and feeling on to the world that surrounds it; and the world, in turn, fixes them, regulates them, and assigns them limits in time.

The hypothesis we have advanced above seems confirmed by the fact that in the very societies where the custom of secondary burial is predominant certain categories of people are purposely excluded from the normal funeral ritual.

This is the case, firstly, with children. The Olo Maanyan place a child less than seven years old in a coffin which will not be changed and which they carry to the family burial place the very day of the death. A sacrifice performed the next day suffices to enable the soul, purified, to enter the realm of the dead at once. The mourning of even the father and mother lasts only a week.[328] But the most common practice among the Dayak and the Papuans seems to be to enclose the bodies of small children inside a tree or to hang them in branches.[329] The concept underlying this custom is clearly revealed to us by the Dayak of Kutai: they believe that men come from the trees and must return there. That is why when a Bahau woman bears a premature child, or if she has been tormented by bad dreams during pregnancy, she can refuse the child by returning it to the tree that it has left either too early or in a worrying fashion.[330] They obviously hope, as is explicitly stated of other peoples,[331] that the soul will soon be reincarnated, perhaps in the womb of the same woman, and will this time make a more auspicious entry into this world. The deaths of children thus provoke only a very weak social reaction which is almost instantaneously completed. It is as though, for the collective consciousness, there were no real death in this case.[332]

Indeed, since the children have not yet entered the visible society, there is no reason to exclude them from it slowly and painfully. As they have not really been separated from the world of spirits, they return there directly,[333] without any sacred energies needing to be called upon, and without a period of painful transition appearing necessary. The death of a new-born child is, at most, an infra-social event; since society has not yet given anything of itself to the child, it is not affected by its disappearance and remains indifferent.

In various Australian tribes, old people who, because of their great age, are incapable of taking part in the totemic ceremonies, who have lost their aptitude for sacred functions, are buried immediately after death instead of being exposed on a platform till the complete desiccation of their bones, as are other members of the tribe.[334] This is so because, due to the weakening of their faculties, they have ceased to participate in social life; their death merely consecrates an exclusion from society which has in fact already been completed,[335] and which every one has had time to get used to.[336]

Finally, the type of death also causes numerous exceptions to the normal ritual. All those who die a violent death or by an accident, women dying in childbirth, people killed by drowning or by lightning, and suicides, are often the object of special rites. Their bodies inspire the most intense horror and are got rid of precipitately; furthermore, their bones are not laid with those of other deceased members of the group who have died a normal death.[337] Their unquiet and spiteful souls roam the earth for ever;[338] or, if they emigrate to another world, they live in a separate village, sometimes even in a completely different area from that inhabited by other souls.[339] It seems, in the most typical cases at least, that the transitory period extends indefinitely for these victims of a special malediction and that their death has no end.[340]

In cases of this kind it is not weakness of the emotion felt by the group which opposes the performance of normal funeral rites, but on the contrary it is the extreme intensity and suddenness of this emotion. An analogy throws more light upon this phenomenon. We have seen that birth, like death, frees dangerous forces which make mother and child taboo for a while. Usually these forces gradually disperse and the mother can be freed. But if the event occurs in an unusual fashion—for instance, if twins are born—then, according to the illuminating expression of the Ba-Ronga, 'this birth is death',[341] for it excludes from normal

life those who seem fated to such a birth. It endows them
with a sacred character of such strength that no rite will
ever be able to efface it, and it throws the entire community
into a state of terror and consternation.[342] Similarly, the
sinister way in which some individuals are torn from this
world separates them for ever from their relatives: their
exclusion is final and irremediable. For it is the last sight of
the individual, as he was when death struck him down,
which impresses itself most deeply on the memory of the
living. This image, because of its uniqueness and its emotional content, can never be completely erased. So it is pointless
to wait a certain period of time in order then to reunite the
deceased with his ancestors; reunion being impossible, delay
is senseless; death will be eternal, because society will always
maintain towards these accursed individuals the attitude of
exclusion that it adopted from the first.

The explanation we propose enables us therefore to
understand at the same time why in a given society double
burial rites are practised, and why in certain cases they are
not.

Let us sum up briefly the results of our investigations.
For the collective consciousness death is in normal circumstances a temporary exclusion of the individual from
human society. This exclusion effects his passage from the
visible society of the living into the invisible society of the
dead. Mourning, at its origin, is the necessary participation
of the living in the mortuary state of their relative, and
lasts as long as this state itself. In the final analysis, death as a
social phenomenon consists in a dual and painful process of
mental disintegration and synthesis. It is only when this
process is completed that society, its peace recovered, can
triumph over death.

THE PRE-EMINENCE
OF THE RIGHT HAND

THE PRE-EMINENCE OF THE RIGHT HAND: A STUDY IN RELIGIOUS POLARITY*

WHAT resemblance more perfect than that between our two hands! And yet what a striking inequality there is!

To the right hand go honours, flattering designations, prerogatives: it acts, orders, and *takes*. The left hand, on the contrary, is despised and reduced to the rôle of a humble auxiliary: by itself it can do nothing; it helps, it supports, it *holds*.

The right hand is the symbol and model of all aristocracy, the left hand of all common people.

What are the titles of nobility of the right hand? And whence comes the servitude of the left?

I. ORGANIC ASYMMETRY

Every social hierarchy claims to be founded on the nature of things, φύσει, οὐ νόμῳ; it thus accords itself eternity, it escapes change and the attacks of innovators. Aristotle justified slavery by the ethnic superiority of the Greeks over barbarians; and today the man who is annoyed by feminist claims alleges that woman is *naturally* inferior. Similarly, according to common opinion, the pre-eminence of the right hand results directly from the organism and owes nothing to convention or to men's changing beliefs. But in spite of appearances the testimony of nature is no more clear or decisive, when it is a question of ascribing attributes to the two hands, than in the conflict of races or the sexes.

* 'La prééminence de la main droite: étude sur la polarité religieuse', *Revue Philosophique*, Vol. LXVIII, 1909, pp. 553–580.

It is not that attempts have been lacking to assign an anatomical cause to right-handedness. Of all the hypotheses advanced[1] only one seems to have stood up to factual test: that which links the preponderance of the right hand to the greater development in man of the left cerebral hemisphere, which, as we know, innervates the muscles of the oposite side. Just as the centre for articulate speech is found in this part of the brain, so the centres which govern voluntary movements are also mainly there. As Broca says, ' We are right-handed because we are left-brained.' The prerogative of the right hand would then be founded on the asymmetric structure of the nervous centres, of which the cause, whatever it may be, is evidently organic.[2]

It is not to be doubted that a regular connection exists between the predominance of the right hand and the superior development of the left part of the brain.* But of these two phenomena which is the cause and which the effect? What is there to prevent us turning Broca's proposition round and saying, 'We are left-brained because we are right-handed?'[3] It is a known fact that the exercise of an organ leads to the greater nourishment and consequent growth of that organ. The greater activity of the right hand, which involves more intensive work for the left nervous centres, has the necessary effect of favouring its development.[4] If we abstract the effects produced by exercise and acquired habits, the physiological superiority of the left hemisphere is reduced to so little that it can at the most determine a slight preference in favour of the right side.

The difficulty that is experienced in assigning a certain and adequate organic cause to the asymmetry of the upper

* [Recent investigation has led to the finding by one anatomist that: 'Although there is a functional asymmetry of the brain, in that the main speech centres tend to be situated in the left cerebral hemisphere, it is extremely doubtful whether there is any significant difference in the mass of the cerebral hemispheres. The conclusion must, therefore, be reached that cranial and cerebral asymmetry are not associated with handedness. . . .' (G. B. D. Scott, 'Cranial and cerebral asymmetry and handedness', *Man*, Vol. 55, 1955, pp. 67–70.)—R. N.]

limbs, joined to the fact that the animals most closely related to man are ambidextrous,[5] has led some authors to disclaim any anatomical basis for the privilege of the right hand. This privilege would not then be inherent in the structure of *genus homo* but would owe its origin exclusively to conditions exterior to the organism.[6]

This radical denial is for the less bold. Doubtless the organic cause of right-handedness is dubious and insufficient, and difficult to distinguish from influences which act on the individual from outside and shape him; but this is no reason for dogmatically denying the action of the physical factor. Moreover, in some cases where external influence and organic tendency are in conflict, it is possible to affirm that the unequal skill of the hands is connected with an anatomical cause. In spite of the forcible and sometimes cruel pressure which society exerts from their childhood on people who are left-handed, they retain all their lives an instinctive preference for the use of the left hand.[7] If we are forced to recognise here the presence of a congenital disposition to asymmetry we must admit that, inversely, for a certain number of people, the preponderant use of the right hand results from the structure of their bodies. The most probable view may be expressed, though not very rigorously, in mathematical form: in a hundred persons there are about two who are naturally left-handed, resistant to any contrary influence; a considerably larger proportion are right-handed by heredity; while between these two extremes oscillate the mass of people, who if left to themselves would be able to use either hand equally, with (in general) a slight preference in favour of the right.[8] There is thus no need to deny the existence of organic tendencies towards asymmetry; but apart from some exceptional cases the vague disposition to right-handedness, which seems to be spread throughout the human species, would not be enough to bring about the absolute preponderance of the right hand if this were not reinforced and fixed by influences extraneous to the organism.

But even if it were established that the right hand surpassed the left, by a gift of nature, in tactile sensibility,
strength and competence, there would still remain to be
explained why a humanly-instituted privilege should be
added to this natural superiority, why only the best-endowed
hand is exercised and trained. Would not reason advise the
attempt to correct by education the weakness of the less
favoured? Quite on the contrary, the left hand is repressed
and kept inactive, its development methodically thwarted.
Dr Jacobs tells us that in the course of his tours of medical
inspection in the Netherlands Indies he often observed that
native children had the left arm completely bound: it was
to teach them *not to use it.*[9] We have abolished material
bonds—but that is all.   One of the signs which distinguish
a well brought-up child is that its left hand has become
incapable of any independent action.

Can it be said that any effort to develop the aptitude
of the left hand is doomed to failure in advance? Experience
shows the contrary. In the rare cases in which the left hand
is properly exercised and trained, because of technical
necessity, it is just about as useful as the right; for example,
in playing the piano or violin, or in surgery. If an accident
deprives a man of his right hand, the left acquires after
some time the strength and skill that it lacked. The example
of people who are left-handed is even more conclusive,
since this time education struggles against the instinctive
tendency to 'unidexterity' instead of following and strength-
ening it. The consequence is that left-handers are generally
ambidextrous and are often noted for their skill.[10] This
result would be attained, with even greater reason, by the
majority of people, who have no irresistible preference for
one side or the other and whose left hand asks only to be
used. The methods of bimanual education, which have
been applied for some years, particularly in English and
American schools, have already shown conclusive results:[11]
there is nothing against the left hand receiving an artistic

and technical training similar to that which has up to now been the monopoly of the right.

So it is not because the left hand is weak and powerless that it is neglected: the contrary is true. This hand is subjected to a veritable mutilation, which is none the less marked because it affects the function and not the outer form of the organ, because it is physiological and not anatomical. The feelings of a left-hander in a backward society[12] are analogous to those of an uncircumcised man in countries where circumcision is law. The fact is that right-handedness is not simply accepted, submitted to, like a natural necessity: it is an ideal to which everybody must conform and which society forces us to respect by positive sanctions. The child which actively uses its left hand is reprimanded, when it is not slapped on the over-bold hand: similarly the fact of being left-handed is an offence which draws on the offender a more or less explicit social reproof.

Organic asymmetry in man is at once a fact and an ideal. Anatomy accounts for the fact to the extent that it results from the structure of the organism; but however strong a determinant one may suppose it to be, it is incapable of explaining the origin of the ideal or the reason for its existence.

2. RELIGIOUS POLARITY

The preponderance of the right hand is obligatory, imposed by coercion, and guaranteed by sanctions: contrarily, a veritable prohibition weighs on the left hand and paralyses it. The difference in value and function between the two sides of our body possesses therefore in an extreme degree the characteristics of a social institution; and a study which tries to account for it belongs to sociology. More precisely, it is a matter of tracing the genesis of an imperative which is half esthetic, half moral. Now the secularised ideas which still dominate our conduct have been born in a mystical form, in the realm of beliefs and religious emotions. We have therefore to seek the explanation of the preference for the right hand in a comparative study of collective representations.[13]

One fundamental opposition dominates the spiritual world of primitive men, that between the sacred and the profane.[14] Certain beings or objects, by virtue of their nature or by the performance of rites, are as it were impregnated with a special essence which consecrates them, sets them apart, and bestows extraordinary powers on them, but which then subjects them to a set of rules and narrow restrictions. Things and persons which are denied this mystical quality have no power, no dignity: they are common and, except for the absolute interdiction on coming into contact with what is sacred, free. Any contact or confusion of beings and things belonging to the opposed classes would be baneful to both. Hence the multitude of prohibitions and taboos which, by keeping them separate, protect both worlds at once.

The significance of the antithesis between profane and sacred varies according to the position in the religious sphere of the mind which classifies beings and evaluates them. Supernatural powers are not all of the same order: some work in harmony with the nature of things, and inspire veneration and confidence by their regularity and majesty; others, on the contrary, violate and disturb the order of the universe, and the respect they impose is founded chiefly on aversion and fear. All these powers have in common the character of being opposed to the profane, to which they are all equally dangerous and forbidden. Contact with a corpse produces in a profane being the same effects as sacrilege. In this sense Robertson Smith was right when he said that the notion of *taboo* comprised simultaneously the sacred and the impure, the divine and the demoniac. But the perspective of a religious world changes when it is regarded no longer from the point of view of the profane but from that of the sacred. The confusion that Robertson Smith referred to no longer exists. A Polynesian chief, for example, knows very well that the religious quality which imbues a corpse is radically contrary to that which he himself possesses. The impure is separated from the sacred and is placed at the opposite pole of the religious universe. On the other hand, from this point of view the profane is no longer defined by purely negative features: it appears as the antagonistic element which by its very contact degrades, diminishes, and changes the essence of things that are sacred. It is a nothingness, as it were, but an active and contagious nothingness: the harmful influence that it exerts on things endowed with sanctity does not differ in intensity from that of baneful powers. There is an imperceptible transition between the lack of sacred powers and the possession of sinister powers.[15] Thus in the classification which has dominated religious consciousness from the beginning and in increasing measure there is a natural affinity and almost an equivalence between the profane and the impure. The two notions are combined and, in opposition to the sacred, form the negative pole of the spiritual universe.

Dualism, which is of the essence of primitive thought, dominates primitive social organisation.[16] The two moieties or phratries which constitute the tribe are reciprocally opposed as sacred and profane. Everything that exists within my own phratry is sacred and forbidden to me: this is why I cannot eat my totem, or spill the blood of a member of my phratry, or even touch his corpse, or marry in my clan. Contrarily, the opposite moiety is profane to me: the clans which compose it supply me with provisions, wives, and human sacrificial victims, bury my dead and prepare my sacred ceremonies.[17] Given the religious character with which the primitive community feels itself invested, the existence of an opposed and complementary section of the same tribe, which can freely carry out functions which are forbidden to members of the first group, is a necessary condition of social life.[18] The evolution of society replaces this reversible dualism with a rigid hierarchical structure:[19] instead of separate and equivalent clans there appear classes or castes, of which one, at the summit, is essentially sacred, noble, and devoted to superior works, while another, at the bottom, is profane or unclean and engaged in base tasks. The principle by which men are assigned rank and function remains the same: social polarity is still a reflection and a consequence of religious polarity.

The whole universe is divided into two contrasted spheres: things, beings, and powers attract or repel each other, implicate or exclude each other, according to whether they gravitate towards one or the other of the two poles.

Powers which maintain and increase life, which give health, social pre-eminence, courage in war and skill in work, all reside in the sacred principle. Contrarily, the profane (in so far as it infringes on the sacred sphere) and the impure are essentially weakening and deadly: the baleful influences which oppress, diminish and harm individuals come from this side. So on one side there is the pole of strength, good, and life; while on the other there is the pole of weakness, evil, and death. Or, if a more recent terminology is preferred, on one side gods, on the other demons.

All the oppositions presented by nature exhibit this fundamental dualism. Light and dark, day and night, east and south in opposition to west and north, represent in imagery and localise in space the two contrary classes of supernatural powers: on one side life shines forth and rises, on the other it descends and is extinguished. The same with the contrast between high and low, sky and earth: on high, the sacred residence of the gods and the stars which know no death; here below, the profane region of mortals whom the earth engulfs; and, lower still, the dark places where lurk serpents and the host of demons.[20]

Primitive thought attributes a sex to all beings in the universe and even to inanimate objects; all of them are divided into two immense classes according to whether they are considered as male or female. Among the Maori the expression *tama tane*, 'male side', designates the most diverse things: men's virility, descent in the paternal line, the east, creative force, offensive magic, and so on; while the expression *tama wahine*, 'female side', covers everything that is the contrary of these.[21] This cosmic distinction rests on a primordial religious antithesis. In general, man is sacred, woman is profane: excluded from ceremonies, she is admitted to them only for a function characteristic of her status, when a taboo is to be lifted, i.e. to bring about an intended profanation.[22] But if woman is powerless and passive in the religious order, she has her revenge in the domain of magic: she is particularly fitted for works of sorcery. 'All evils, misery, and death', says a Maori proverb, 'come from the female element.' Thus the two sexes correspond to the sacred and to the profane (or impure), to life and to death. An abyss separates them, and a rigorous division of labour apportions activities between men and women in such a way that there can never be mixing or confusion.[23]

If dualism marks the entire thought of primitive men, it influences no less their religious activity, their worship. This influence is nowhere more manifest than in the *tira* ceremony, which occurs very often in Maori ritual and serves the most diverse ends. The priest makes two small mounds on a sacred plot of ground, of which one, the male, is dedicated to the Sky, and the other, the female, to the Earth. On each of them he erects a stick: one, called the 'wand of life' and which is placed to the east, is the emblem and focus of health, strength, and life; the other, which is placed to the west, is the 'wand of death' and is the emblem and focus of all evil. The detail of the rites varies according to the end sought, but the fundamental theme is always the same: on

G

the one hand, to repel towards the pole of mortality all impurities and evils which have penetrated and which threaten the community; on the other, to secure, strengthen, and attract to the tribe the beneficent influences which reside at the pole of life. At the end of the ceremony the priest knocks down the wand of Earth, leaving the wand of Sky standing: this is the sought-after triumph of life over death, the expulsion and abolition of evil, the well-being of the community and the ruin of its enemies.[24] Thus ritual activity is directed with reference to two opposite poles, each of which has its essential function in the cult, and which correspond to the two contrary and complementary attitudes of religious life.

How could man's body, the microcosm, escape the law of polarity which governs everything? Society and the whole universe have a side which is sacred, noble and precious, and another which is profane and common: a male side, strong and active, and another, female, weak and passive; or, in two words, a right side and a left side—and yet the human organism alone should be symmetrical? A moment's reflection shows us that that is an impossibility. Such an exception would not only be an inexplicable anomaly, it would ruin the entire economy of the spiritual world. For man is at the centre of creation: it is for him to manipulate and direct for the better the formidable forces which bring life and death. Is it conceivable that all these things and these powers, which are separated and contrasted and are mutually exclusive, should be confounded abominably in the hand of the priest or the artisan? It is a vital necessity that neither of the two hands should know what the other doeth:[25] the evangelical precept merely applies to a particular situation this law of the incompatibility of opposites, which is valid for the whole world of religion.[26]

If organic asymmetry had not existed, it would have had to be invented.

3. THE CHARACTERISTICS OF RIGHT AND LEFT

The different way in which the collective consciousness envisages and values the right and the left appears clearly in language. There is a striking contrast in the words which in most Indo-European languages designate the two sides. While there is a single term for 'right' which extends over a very wide area and shows great stability,[27] the idea of 'left' is expressed by a number of distinct terms, which are less widely spread and seem destined to disappear constantly in the face of new words.[28] Some of these words are obvious euphemisms,[29] others are of extremely obscure origin. 'It seems', says Meillet,[30] 'that when speaking of the left side one avoided pronouncing the proper word and tended to replace it by different ones which were constantly renewed.' The multiplicity and instability of terms for the left, and their evasive and arbitrary character, may be explained by the sentiments of disquiet and aversion felt by the community with respect to the left side.[31] Since the thing itself could not be changed the name for it was, in the hope of abolishing or reducing the evil. But in vain; for even words with happy meanings, when applied by antiphrasis to the left, are quickly contaminated by what they express and acquire a 'sinister' quality which soon forbids their use. Thus the opposition which exists between right and left is seen even in the different natures and destinies of their names.

The same contrast appears if we consider the meaning of the words 'right' and 'left'. The former is used to express ideas of physical strength and 'dexterity', of intellectual 'rectitude' and good judgement, of 'uprightness' and moral integrity, of good fortune and beauty, of juridical norm; while the word 'left' evokes most of the ideas contrary to these. To unite these many meanings, it is ordinarily supposed that the word 'right' meant first of all our better hand, then 'the qualities of strength and skill which are natural to it', and by extension diverse analogous virtues of the mind and heart.[32] But this is an arbitrary construction. There is nothing to authorise the statement that the ancient Indo-European word for the right first had an exclusively physical connotation; and more recently formed words such as our *droit*[33] and the Armenian *adj*,[34] before being applied to one of the sides of the body, expressed the idea of a force which goes straight to its object, by ways which are normal and certain, in opposition to ways which are tortuous, oblique, and abortive. In fact, the different meanings of the word in our languages, which are the products of an advanced civilisation, are distinct and juxtaposed. If we trace them back by the comparative method to the source from which these fragmentary meanings derive, we find them fused together originally in one notion which encompasses and confounds them all. We have already met this notion: for the right, it is the idea of sacred power, regular and beneficent, the principle of all effective activity, the source of everything that is good, favourable and legitimate; for the left, this ambiguous conception of the profane and the impure, the feeble and incapable which is also maleficent and dreaded. Physical strength (or weakness) here is only a particular and derivative aspect of a much more vague and fundamental quality.

Among the Maori the right is the sacred side, the seat of good and creative powers; the left is the profane side, possessing no virtue other than, as we shall see, certain disturbing and suspect powers.[35] The same contrast reappears in the course of the evolution of religion, in more precise and less impersonal forms: the right is the side of the gods, where hovers the white figure of a good guardian angel; the left side is dedicated to demons, the devil; a black and wicked angel holds it in dominion.[36] Even today, if the right hand is still called good and beautiful and the left bad and ugly,[37] we can discern in these childish expressions the weakened echoes of designations and religious emotions which for many centuries have been attached to the two sides of our body.

It is a notion current among the Maori that the right is the 'side of life' (and of strength) while the left is the 'side of death' (and of weakness).[38] Fortunate and life-giving influences enter us from the right and through our right side; and, inversely, death and misery penetrate to the core of our being from the left.[39] So the resistance of the side which is particularly exposed and defenceless has to be strengthened by protective amulets; the ring that we wear on the third finger of the left hand is primarily intended to keep temptations and other bad things from us.[40] Hence the great importance in divination of distinguishing the sides, both of the body and in space. If I have felt a convulsive tremor while sleeping it is a sign that a spirit has seized me, and according to whether the sign was on the right or on the left I can expect good fortune and life or ill-fortune and death.[41] The same rule holds in general for omens which consist in the appearance of animals thought to be bearers of fate: sometimes these messages are susceptible of two contradictory interpretations, according to whether the situation is seen from the point of view of the person who sees the animal or of the animal which he encounters;[42] if it appears on the left it presents its right side, therefore it can be considered favourable. But these divergences, carefully maintained by the augurs for the confusion of the common people and the increase of their own prestige, only show in a still clearer light the affinity that exists between the right and life, and between the left and death.

A no less significant concordance links the sides of the body to regions in space. The right represents what is high, the upper world, the sky; while the left is connected with the underworld and the earth.[43] It is not by chance that in pictures of the Last Judgement it is the Lord's raised right hand that indicates their sublime abode to the elect, while his lowered left hand shows the damned the gaping jaws of

Hell ready to swallow them. The relation uniting the right to the east or south and the left to the north or west is even more constant and direct, to the extent that in many languages the same words denote the sides of the body and the cardinal points.[44] The axis which divides the world into two halves, the one radiant and the other dark, also cuts through the human body and divides it between the empire of light and that of darkness.[45] Right and left extend beyond the limits of our body to embrace the universe.

According to a very widespread idea, at least in the Indo-European area, the community forms a closed circle at the centre of which is the altar, the Ark of the Covenant, where the gods descend and from which divine aid radiates. Order and harmony reign within the enclosure, while outside it extends a vast night, limitless and lawless, full of impure germs and traversed by chaotic forces. On the periphery of the sacred space the worshippers make a ritual circuit round the divine centre, their right shoulders turned towards it.[46] They have everything to hope for from one side, everything to fear from the other. The right is the *inside*, the finite, assured well-being, and peace; the left is the *outside*, the infinite, hostile, and the perpetual menace of evil.

The above equivalents would in themselves allow us to assume that the right side and the male element are of the same nature, and likewise the left side and the female element; but we are not reduced to simple conjecture on this point. The Maori apply the terms *tama tane* and *tama wahine* to the two sides of the body, terms whose almost universal extension we have already noted: man is compounded of two natures, masculine and feminine; the former is attributed to the right side, the latter to the left.[47] Among the Wulwanga tribe of Australia two sticks are used to mark the beat during ceremonies: one is called the man and is held in the right hand, while the other, the woman, is held in the left. Naturally, it is always the 'man' which strikes and

the 'woman' which receives the blows; the right which
acts, the left which submits.[48] Here we find intimately
combined the privilege of the strong sex and that of the
strong side. Undoubtedly God took one of Adam's left
ribs to create Eve, for one and the same essence characterises
woman and the left side of the body. It is a matter of the
two parts of a weak and defenceless being, somewhat
ambiguous and disquieting, destined by nature to a passive
and receptive rôle and to a subordinate position.[49]

Thus the opposition of the right and the left has the same
meaning and application as the series of contrasts, very
different but reducible to common principles, presented
by the universe. Sacred power, source of life, truth, beauty,
virtue, the rising sun, the male sex, and—I can add—the
right side; all these terms are interchangeable, as are their
contraries, they designate under many aspects the same
category of things, a common nature, the same orientation
towards one of the two poles of the mystical world.[50] Can one
believe that a slight difference of degree in the physical
strength of the two hands could be enough to account for
such a trenchant and profound heterogeneity?

4. THE FUNCTIONS OF THE TWO HANDS

The different characteristics of the right and the left
determine the difference in rank and functions which exists
between the two hands.

It is well known that many primitive peoples, particularly
the Indians of North America, can converse without saying
a word, simply by movements of the head and arms. In
this language each hand acts in accordance with its nature.
The right hand stands for *me*, the left for *not-me, others*.[51] To
express the idea of *high* the right hand is raised above the
left, which is held horizontal and motionless; while the idea of
low is expressed by lowering the 'inferior hand' below the
right.[52] The raised right hand signifies *bravery, power, virility;*

while on the contrary the same hand, turned to the left and placed below the left hand, signifies, according to context, the ideas of *death, destruction* and *burial*.[53] These characteristic examples are enough to show that the contrast between right and left, and the relative positions of the hands, are of fundamental importance in 'sign-language'.

The hands are used only incidentally for the expression of ideas: they are primarily instruments with which man acts on the beings and things that surround him. It is in the diverse fields of human activity that we must observe the hands at work.

In worship man seeks above all to communicate with sacred powers, in order to maintain and increase them, and to draw to himself the benefits of their action. Only the right hand is fit for these beneficial relations, since it participates in the nature of the things and beings on which the rites are to act. The gods are on our right, so we turn towards the right to pray.[54] A holy place must be entered right foot first.[55] Sacred offerings are presented to the gods with the right hand.[56] It is the right hand that receives favours from heaven and which transmits them in the benediction.[57] To bring about good effects in a ceremony, to bless or to consecrate, the Hindus and the Celts go three times round a person or an object, from left to right, like the sun, with the right side turned inwards. In this way they pour upon whatever is enclosed in the sacred circle the holy and beneficent virtue which emanates from the right side. The contrary movement and position, in similar circumstances, would be sacrilegious and unlucky.[58]

But worship does not consist entirely in the trusting adoration of friendly gods. Man would willingly forget the sinister powers which swarm at his left, but he cannot; for they impose themselves on his attention by their murderous blows, by threats which must be eluded, and demands which must be satisfied. A considerable part of a religious cult, and not the least important part, is devoted to containing or appeasing spiteful or angry supernatural beings, to banishing and destroying bad influences. In this domain it is the left hand that prevails: it is directly concerned with all that is demoniacal.[59] In the Maori ceremony that we described it is the left hand that sets up and then knocks down the wand of death.[60] If greedy spirits of the souls of the dead have to be placated by the making of a gift, it is the left hand that is specified for this sinister contact.[61] Sinners are expelled from the Church by the left door.[62] In funerary rites and in exorcism the ceremonial circuit is made 'in the wrong direction', presenting the left side.[63] Is it not right that the destructive powers of the left side should sometimes be turned against the malicious spirits who themselves generally use them?

Magical practices proliferate on the borders of regular liturgy. The left hand is at home here: it excels at neutralising or annulling bad fortune,[64] but above all in propagating death.[65] 'When you drink with a native [on the Guinea Coast] you must watch his left hand, for the very contact of his left thumb with the drink would suffice to make it fatal.' It is said that every native conceals under his left thumb-nail a toxic substance that possesses almost 'the devastating subtlety of prussic acid'.[66] This poison, which is evidently imaginary, symbolises perfectly the murderous powers that lie in the left side.

It is clear that there is no question here of strength or weakness, of skill or clumsiness, but of different and in-compatible functions linked to contrary natures. If the left hand is despised and humiliated in the world of the gods and of the living, it has its domain where it is mistress and from which the right hand is excluded; but this is a dark and ill-famed region. The power of the left hand is always somewhat occult and illegitimate; it inspires terror and repulsion. Its movements are suspect; we should like it to remain quiet and discreet, hidden in the folds of the garment, so that its corruptive influence will not spread.

As people in mourning, whom death has enveloped, have to veil themselves, neglect their bodies, let their hair and nails grow, so it would be out of place to take too much care of the bad hand: the nails are not cut and it is washed less than the other.[67] Thus the belief in a profound disparity between the two hands sometimes goes so far as to produce a visible bodily asymmetry. Even if it is not betrayed by its appearance, the left still remains the cursed hand. A left hand that is too gifted and agile is the sign of a nature contrary to right order, of a perverse and devilish disposition: every left-handed person is a possible sorcerer, justly to be distrusted.[68] To the contrary, the exclusive preponderance of the right, and a repugnance for requiring anything of the left, are the marks of a soul unusually associated with the divine and immune to what is profane or impure: such are the Christian saints who in their cradle were pious to the extent of refusing the left breast of their mother.[69] This is why social selection favours right-handers and why education is directed to paralysing the left hand while developing the right.

Life in society involves a large number of practices which, without being integrally part of religion, are closely connected with it. If it is the right hands that are joined in a marriage, if the right hand takes the oath, concludes contracts, takes possession, and lends assistance, it is because it is in man's right side that lie the powers and authority which give weight to the gestures, the force by which it exercises its hold on things.[70] How could the left hand conclude valid acts since it is deprived of prestige and spiritual power, since it has strength only for destruction and evil? Marriage contracted with the left hand is a clandestine and irregular union from which only bastards can issue. The left is the hand of perjury, treachery, and fraud.[71] As with jural formalities, so also the rules of etiquette derive directly from worship: the gestures with which we adore the gods serve also to express the feelings of respect and affectionate esteem that we have for one another.[72] In greeting and in friendship we offer the best we have, our right.[73] The king bears the emblems of his sovereignty on his right side, he places at his right those whom he judges most worthy to receive, without polluting them, the precious emanations from his right side. It is because the right and the left are really of different value and dignity that it means so much to present the one or the other to our guests, according to their position in the social heirarchy.[74] All these usages, which today seem to be pure conventions, are explained and acquire meaning if they are related to the beliefs which gave birth to them.

Let us look more closely at the profane. Many primitive peoples, when they are in a state of impurity—during mourning, for example—may not use their hands, and in particular they may not use them for eating. They must be fed by others putting the food into their mouths, or they seize the food in their mouths like dogs, since if they touched the food with their polluted hands they would swallow their own death.[75] In this case a sort of mystical infirmity affects both hands and for a time paralyses them. It is a prohibition of the same order that bears on the left hand, but as it is of the same nature as this hand itself the paralysis is permanent. This is why very commonly only the right hand can be actively used at meals. Among the tribes of the lower Niger it is even forbidden for women to use their left hands when cooking, evidently under pain of being accused of attempted poisoning and sorcery.[76] The left hand, like those pariahs on whom all impure tasks are thrust, may concern itself only with disgusting duties.[77] We are far from the sanctuary here; but the dominion of religious concepts is so powerful that it makes itself felt in the dining-room, the kitchen, and even in those places haunted by demons and which we dare not name.

It seems, however, that there is one order of activity at least which escapes mystical influences, viz. the arts and industry: the different rôles of right and left in these are held to be connected entirely with physical and utilitarian

causes. But such a view fails to recognise the character of
techniques in antiquity: these were impregnated with re-
ligiosity and dominated by mystery. What more sacred for
primitive man than war or the hunt! These entail the
possession of special powers and a state of sanctity that is
difficult to acquire and still more difficult to preserve. The
weapon itself is a sacred thing, endowed with a power which
alone makes blows directed at the enemy effective. Unhappy
the warrior who profanes his spear or sword and dissipates
its virtue! Is it possible to entrust something so precious to
the left hand? This would be monstrous sacrilege, as much
as it would be to allow a woman to enter the warriors'
camp, i.e. to doom them to defeat and death. It is man's
right side that is dedicated to the god of war; it is the *mana*
of the right shoulder that guides the spear to its target;
it is therefore only the right hand that will carry and wield
the weapon.[78] The left hand, however, is not unemployed:
it provides for the needs of profane life that even an intense
consecration cannot interrupt, and which the right hand,
strictly dedicated to war, must ignore.[79] In battle, without
actually taking part in the action, it can parry the adversary's
blows; its nature fits it for defence; it is the shield hand.

The origin of ideas about right and left has often been
sought in the different rôles of the two hands in battle, a
difference resulting from the structure of the organism or
from a sort of instinct.[80] This hypothesis, refuted by decisive
arguments,[81] takes for the cause what is really the effect.
It is none the less true that the warlike functions of the two
hands have sometimes reinforced the characteristics already
attributed to them and the relations of one to the other.
Consider an agricultural people who prefer peaceful works
to pillage and conquest, and who never have recourse to
arms except in defence: the 'shield hand' will rise in popular
estimation, while the 'spear hand' will lose something of its
prestige. This is notably the case among the Zuni, who
personify the left and right sides of the body as two gods who

are brothers: the former, the elder, is reflective, wise, and of sound judgement; while the latter is impetuous, impulsive, and made for action.[82] But however interesting this secondary development may be, which considerably modifies the characteristic features of the two sides, it must not make us forget the primary religious significance of the contrast between the right and the left.

What is true of military art applies also to other techniques; but a valuable account from the Maori enables us to see directly what makes the right hand preponderant in human industry. The account concerns the initiation of a young girl into the craft of weaving, a serious affair wrapped in mystery and full of danger. The apprentice sits in the presence of the master, who is both artisan and priest, in front of two carved posts which are stuck in the ground and form a sort of rudimentary loom. In the right post lie the sacred virtues which constitute the art of weaving and which make the work effectual; the left post is profane and empty of any power. While the priest recites his incantations the apprentice bites the right post in order to absorb its essence and consecrate herself to her vocation. Naturally, only the right hand comes into contact with the sacred post, the profanation of which would be fatal to the initiate; and it is the same hand that carries the thread, which is also sacred, from left to right. As for the profane hand, it can co-operate only humbly and at a distance in the solemn work that is done.[83] Doubtless this division of labour is relaxed in the case of rougher and more profane pursuits. But none the less it remains the case that, as a rule, techniques consist in setting in motion, by delicate manipulation, dangerous mystical forces: only the sacred and effective hand can take the risk of initiative; if the baneful hand actively intervenes it will only dry up the source of success and vitiate the work that is undertaken.[84]

Thus, from one end to the other of the world of humanity, in the sacred places where the worshipper meets his god, in the cursed places where devilish pacts are made, on the throne as well as in the witness-box, on the battlefield and in the peaceful workroom of the weaver, everywhere one unchangeable law governs the functions of the two hands. No more than the profane is allowed to mix with the sacred is the left allowed to trespass on the right. A preponderant activity of the bad hand could only be illegitimate or exceptional; for it would be the end of man and everything else if the profane were ever allowed to prevail over the sacred and death over life. The supremacy of the right hand is at once an effect and a necessary condition of the order which governs and maintains the universe.

5. CONCLUSION

Analysis of the characteristics of the right and the left, and the functions attributed to them, has confirmed the thesis of which deduction gave us a glimpse. The obligatory differentiation between the sides of the body is a particular case and a consequence of the dualism which is inherent in primitive thought. But the religious necessities which make the pre-eminence of one of the hands inevitable do not determine which of them will be preferred. How is it that the sacred side should invariably be the right and the profane the left?

According to some authors the differentiation of right and left is completely explained by the rules of religious orientation and sun-worship. The position of man in space is neither indifferent nor arbitrary. In his prayers and ceremonies the worshipper looks naturally to the region where the sun rises, the source of all life. Most sacred buildings, in different religions, are turned towards the east. Given this direction, the parts of the body are themselves assigned to cardinal points: west is behind, south to the right, and the north to the left. Consequently the characteristics of the heavenly regions are reflected in the human body. The full sunlight of the south shines on our right side, while the sinister shade of the north is projected to our left. The spectacle of nature, the contrast of daylight and darkness, of heat and cold, are held to have taught man to distinguish and to oppose his right and his left.[85]

This explanation rests on outmoded ideas about naturalistic conceptions. The external world, with its light and shade, enriches and gives precision to religious notions which issue from the depths of the collective consciousness; but it does not create them. It would be easy to formulate the same hypothesis in more correct terms and to restrict its application to the point that we are concerned with; but it would still run up against contrary facts of a decisive nature.[86] In fact, there is nothing to allow us to assert that the distinctions applied to space are anterior to those that concern man's body. They all have one and the same origin, the opposition of the sacred and the profane; therefore they are usually concordant and support each other; but they are not thereby less independent. We must therefore seek in the structure of the organism the dividing line which directs the beneficent flow of supernatural favours towards the right side.

This ultimate recourse to anatomy should not be seen as a contradiction or concession. It is one thing to explain the nature and origin of a force, it is another to determine the point at which it is applied. The slight physiological advantages possessed by the right hand are merely the occasion of a qualitative differentiation of which the cause lies beyond the individual, in the constitution of the collective consciousness. An almost insignificant bodily asymmetry is enough to turn in one direction and the other contrary representations which are already completely formed. Thereafter, thanks to the plasticity of the organism, social constraint[87] adds to the opposed members and incorporates in them those qualities of strength and weakness, dexterity and clumsiness,* which in the adult appear to spring spontaneously from nature.[88]

* [Fr. *gaucherie*, lit. 'leftness'.]

The exclusive development of the right hand has sometimes been seen as a characteristic attribute of man and a sign of his moral pre-eminence. In a sense this is true. For centuries the systematic paralysation of the left arm has, like other mutilations, expressed the will animating man to make the sacred predominate over the profane, to sacrifice the desires and the interest of the individual to the demands felt by the collective consciousness, and to spiritualise the body itself by marking upon it the opposition of values and the violent contrasts of the world of morality. It is because man is a double being—*homo duplex*—that he possesses a right and a left that are profoundly differentiated.

This is not the place to seek the cause and the meaning of this polarity which dominates religious life and is imposed on the body itself. This is one of the profoundest questions which the science of comparative religion and sociology in general have to solve; we ought not to tackle it indirectly. Perhaps we have been able to bring certain novel elements into this research; in any case, it is not without interest to see a particular problem reduced to another that is much more general.

As philosophers have often remarked,[89] the distinction between right and left is one of the essential articles of our intellectual equipment. It seems impossible, then, to explain the meaning and genesis of this distinction without taking the part, at least implicitly, of one or the other traditional doctrines of the origin of knowledge.

What disputes there were formerly between the partisans of innate distinction and those of experience! And what a fine clash of dialectical arguments! The application of experimental and sociological method to human problems puts an end to this conflict of dogmatic and contradictory assertions. Those who believe in the innate capacity to differentiate have won their victory: the intellectual and moral representations of right and left are true categories, anterior to all individual experience, since they are linked to the very structure of social thought. But the advocates of experience were right too, for there is no question here of immutable instincts or of absolute metaphysical data. These categories are transcendent only in relation to the individual: placed in their original setting, the collective consciousness, they appear as facts of nature, subject to change and dependent on complex conditions.

Even if, as it seems, the different attributes of the two hands, the dexterity of one and the clumsiness of the other, are in great part the work of human will, the dream of humanity gifted with two 'right hands' is not visionary. But from the fact that ambidexterity is possible it does not follow that it is desirable; the social causes which led to the differentiation of the two hands might be permanent. However, the evolution that we are now witnessing hardly justifies such a view. The tendency to level the value of the two hands is not an isolated or abnormal fact in our culture. The ancient religious ideas which put unbridgeable distance between things and beings, and which in particular founded the exclusive preponderance of the right hand, are today in full retreat. Neither aesthetics nor morality would suffer from the revolution of supposing that there were weighty physical and technical advantages to mankind in permitting the left hand at least to reach its full development. The distinction of good and evil, which for long was solidary with the antithesis of right and left, will not vanish from our conscience the moment the left hand makes a more effective contribution to human labour and is able, on occasion, to take the place of the right. If the constraint of a mystical ideal has for centuries been able to make man a unilateral being, physiologically mutilated, a liberated and foresighted community will strive to develop better the energies dormant in our left side and in our right cerebral hemisphere, and to assure by an appropriate training a more harmonious development of the organism.

NOTES

NOTES

THE COLLECTIVE REPRESENTATION OF DEATH

[1] Cf. Dastre 1903: 296 ff.

[2] Lafitau 1724, 2: 444.

[3] The institution is relatively well known among them; Grabowsky has collated the accounts relating to the Dayak of the southeast (Olo Ngaju and Ot Danom), together with certain personal observations, in an article that is valuable but a little subject to caution (1889: 177 ff.). It contains a bibliography; the best source remains Hardeland, who has published, as an appendix to his Dayak grammar (1858), the complete text and a literal translation of a large number of songs and formulas recited by the priestesses during the *tivah*.

[4] Cf., on the Olo Ngaju, Grabowsky (1889: 182); on the Olo Maanyan, Tromp (1877: 48); on the Dayak of Kutai, Tromp (1888: 76) and Bock (1881: 141–2); on the Kayan, a riverine people of the Tinjar, Hose in Ling Roth (1896, 1: 148); on the Long Kiput of the Baram river, Kükenthal (1896: 270); on the Skapan, Brooke Low in Roth (1896, 1: 152–3); on the Dusun and Murut of the north of the island, Roth (1896, 1: 151, 153).

[5] Grabowsky 1884: 472; Tromp 1877: 47 ff.

[6] Cf. for example Nieuwenhuis 1907, 1: 27.

[7] Cf. Tromp 1888: 76; according to Müller (1839–44: 402), among the riverine Olo Ngaju of the Beyaju the coffin is placed with a number of others in a collective sepulture, the *sandong raung;* but this report is contradicted by Hardeland (1859: 503), who tells us expressly that the coffin (*raung*) is not taken to the collective resting-place or *sandong* until the time of the final ceremony. In any case, if the example reported by Müller is exact it is exceptional: the rule is that the coffin is isolated during the period of waiting.

[8] Cf. for example Grabowsky 1889: 181–2.

[9] Hardeland 1858: 350; Perelaer 1870: 224–5.

[10] It has the same name among the Olo Ngaju: *pasah;* cf. Hardeland 1859 s.v. Among the Alfuru of north Halmahera the temporary sepulture is called 'the house of the deceased' (Clercq 1889: 208).

[11] Cf. in particular Nieuwenhuis 1907, 1: 162.

[12] In Timor Laut, Riedel (1886: 305–6); on Timor, Forbes (1885: 434); on the Toumbuluh of Minahassa, cf. Riedel (1895: 108–9).

[13] Among the Olo Ngaju there is no burial unless it is foreseen that there will be a long wait before the second obsequies; if the coffin were raised above the ground it would be in danger of falling, an event

considered fatal for the family. A little hut is built over the tomb (Grabowsky 1889: 182). Among the Olo Maanyan, burial is the rule when the corpse is not kept in the house (Tromp 1877: 46).

[14] Halewijn, in Grabowsky 1889: 182.

[15] 1859 s.v. *tiwah*.

[16] Müller 1839–44: 402.

[17] Hardeland 1859.

[18] On Timor, according to Forbes (1885: 434), the delay may sometimes last a whole century (for important chiefs); the obligation to celebrate the final rites is then transmitted from father to son, with the inheritance.

[19] Grabowsky 1889: 188.

[20] As is thought by Wilken (1884: 77 ff.; 1886, 3: 255 ff.; 4: 347 ff.).

[21] Müller 1839–44; Hardeland 1859 s.v. *tiwah*.

[22] Certain authors explain the provisional exposure of the corpse exclusively by the length of time demanded by the essential preparations and the difficulty of procuring victims for the sacrifice: cf., for the Batak, Hagen (1883: 517) and Rosenberg (1878: 27); for the inhabitants of northern Nias, Rosenberg (1878: 156); for Timor, Forbes (1885: 434 ff.); for the Kai Islands, Rosenberg (1878:351).

[23] This is the case notably in Borneo, for the Milanau, the Dusun, and the Murut (Roth 1896, 1: 150–2), for the Long Kiput (Kükenthal 1896: 270); for the riverine Dayak of the Kapuas in western Borneo (Veth 1856, 2: 270); for the Ot Danom (Schwaner 1854: 151); in Sumatra, for the Karo Batak (Hagen 1883: 520); in Timor Laut (Forbes 1885: 322 ff.; Riedel 1886: 305–6); on Buru (Forbes 1885: 405); for the Alfuru of eastern Celebes (Bosscher in Wilken 1884: 179); in northern Halmahera (Clercq 1889: 208); on the island of Babar (Riedel 1886: 359).

[24] To this end a tube of bamboo is passed through a hole bored in the bottom of the coffin; cf. for example, on the Olo Ngaju, Grabowsky (1889: 181); on the Batak, Tuuk (1861: 165); on the Alfuru of the Bolaang-Mongoudou district, Wilken & Schwarz (1867: 323).

[25] Cf. Low 1848: 207: 'The disgusting odour produced by decomposition (as the Dayak have frequently told me) is particularly agreeable to their senses.' This passage concerns the corpse or rather the head of an enemy.

[26] Hardeland 1858: 218 (and the commentary).—Meyer & Richter (1896: 110 n. 1) suggest that the coffin was hermetically sealed perhaps in order to prevent the dreaded exit of the soul of the deceased; they add that the smell of decomposition might have been considered as the sign of the presence of the soul. The text transcribed by Hardeland seems to show that in fact the fear of a mystical danger is the determining motive, and at the same time that it is useless to bring in the idea of the soul of the deceased.

[27] Perham, in Roth (1896, 1: 204, 210), on the subject of the Sea Dayak who practise immediate burial: 'The body of a dead person is not

called body or corpse; it is an *antu* (spirit); and if the living kept it near them for long they would expose themselves to sinister supernatural influences.'

[28] Cf. p. 35.

[29] Grabowsky 1889: 181; according to Salomon Müller (1839–44) the pot is buried at the place where the remains of the corpse have been cremated.

[30] This rather vague statement shows without doubt that in this case the relatives cannot yet be relieved of the taboos and observances of mourning.

[31] Tromp 1877: 48; cf. Grabowsky 1884: 472.

[32] *Relation:* 59; cf. Crawfurd 1820: 255.

[33] Ritter, in Veth (1856, 2: 270).—In order to make the comparison between these western Dayak and the Olo Maanyan more complete we must add that among the latter, during the forty-nine days that precede the strange ceremony we have seen, the closest relatives of the deceased, instead of eating rice, have to eat *jelai:* its grains are small, brown in colour, have a *quite disagreeable smell,* and taste very nasty (Tromp 1877: 44, 47). Does the detail that we have italicised permit us to think that the *jelai* of the Sihing people is the substitute (after the decline of the former custom) for the rice impregnated with matter from the corpse which is imposed on the western Dayak? This hypothesis is not indispensable to our interpretation; the 'duty' in question in the passage above, and in which the relatives must not fail, was to not allow the matter to accumulate in the pot, and to take their share of it. The rite has eventually become an arbitrary formality.—On certain islands of Timor Laut the natives rub their bodies with the liquids coming from the corpses of their close relatives or chiefs (Riedel 1886: 308).

[34] For example, the body of a child for a certain time after its birth, or of a woman during menstruation.

[35] Cf. Nieuwenhuis (1907, 1: 89): he gives as motive the desire to 'appease the evil spirits which might take possession of it'; in the case of chiefs he mentions in addition various protective amulets. Similarly, during certain ceremonies concerned with pregnancy or birth, the most exposed persons stop their ears with cotton 'in order not to be troubled by the evil spirits' (Riedel 1895: 95, 99). It is true that other authors present this custom as intended solely for the protection of the living (Grabowsky 1889: 179). The rite is probably ambiguous, with a dual object, as is often the case: it is concerned simultaneously, and confusedly, with preventing the spread of the fatal influence contained in the corpse, and with barring the way to evil spirits that want to penetrate the corpse and take possession of it. Also, elements of Hindu provenance seem in certain cases to have been grafted on to the original custom.

[36] Tromp 1877: 48; this text concerns the case when the corpse is kept in the house. But in Timor Laut, where it is exposed on the seashore at some distance from the village, figures of men beating gongs, firing

guns, and gesticulating furiously are drawn on the coffin—at least when it concerns a person of mark—in order to frighten away evil influences from the sleeper (Forbes 1885: 322 ff.; cf. Kükenthal 1896: 180).

[37] It is found (exceptionally) among the Olo Ngaju (Hardeland 1859: 233; 1858: 364 n. 223; Braches 1882: 102); among the Olo Maanyan (Grabowsky 1884: 471; Tromp 1877: 47); among the Bahau. (Nieuwenhuis 1907, 1: 104); among the Kayan (Roth 1896, 2: 142); in the Serang Islands (Riedel 1886: 144); and on Bali (van Eck, in Wilken 1884: 52), etc.

[38] Hardeland 1859: 233, 308; Perelaer 1870: 219, 227; Grabowsky 1889: 183 ff.

[39] The same distinction is reported by Nieuwenhuis (1907, 1: 103) among the Bahau; but the two souls are separate even during the lifetime of the individual.

[40] Also the living offer it a sort of material support in their house: a plank covered with figures relating to the last journey of the soul and the other world (cf. Grabowsky 1889: 184).

[41] If the *tivah* cannot be celebrated by the family the soul is in great danger of seeing this temporary state prolonged indefinitely; it is then, according to a characteristic expression, a *liau matai*, a dead soul (Grabowsky 1889: 181).

[42] Kruyt 1895: 24, 26, 28. The author observes that 'the idea of a house of waiting exists even among those for whom the soul stays on earth until the *tengke;* doubtless the soul is believed to pass part of this period on earth and part in the house. The thoughts of the Alfuru on this point are not clear.' But this very vacillation seems to us characteristic, and the two conceptions, which seem logically exclusive, are at bottom interdependent (with no need to separate them in time): it is because he has not yet completely left this world that the deceased cannot yet completely enter the other.

[43] For example, the Ot Danom, who in this regard contrast with their neighbours the Olo Ngaju (Schwaner 1853, 2: 76).

[44] Cf., on the Sea Dayak, Perham (Roth 1896, 1: 203, 206–7, 209); for the Toumbuluh of Minahassa, cf. Riedel (1895: 105–7).

[45] The belief that the soul stays on earth for a time before leaving for the land of the dead is also found among peoples which nowadays bury the body (for good) immediately after death; cf. for example, for the Dayak of the interior, Low (Roth 1896, 1: 217); for the island of Roti, Graafland (1890: 168) and Heijmering (1843: 363 ff.); the period of waiting is simply shorter: nine and twelve days in the two cases cited.

[46] Tromp (1877: 47): in the case of deceased persons whose bodies are kept in the house; for others the obligation is less strict.—Cf. on Sumba, Roos (1872: 58).

[47] Perham (Roth 1896, 1: 209–10); in the morning traces of its passage are sometimes found near the rice.

[48] Forbes 1885: 438, 447—this interregnum may last very long (thirty years or more) because of the great expenses necessitated by the rite.

[49] Thus the Dayak, before dying, begs his relatives not to wait too long before celebrating the *tivah* (Grabowsky 1889: 188).

[50] Grabowsky 1889: 182; cf., for the Tagal of the Philippines, Blumentritt (18: 166–8).

[51] Perham (Roth 1896, 1: 209–10).

[52] Hardeland 1859: 308.

[53] Riedel (on the Toumbuluh) 1895: 107; cf., on the Kayan, Roth 1896, 2: 142. It is not a question here of souls which for one reason or another will never attain the peace and security of the beyond.

[54] It would seem vain to us to try to decide which of these two motives is 'primitive'; this is a misplaced question which can only be decided arbitrarily.

[55] Cf. Riedel 1895: 106–7. The Toumbuluh priests are at once psychopomps and exorcizers who drive out spirits; during the nine days following the ceremony conveying the soul to the land of the dead, they perform a war-dance to frighten it (in the event that it has not yet departed) so that it will not return to torment its relatives.

[56] This distinction would be unfounded if it were necessary to admit the theory formerly propounded by Frazer (1886: 64 ff.); for the mourning practices would only be rites intended to protect the living against the offensive return of the soul of the deceased; but this theory was too narrow and artificial. The view that we adopt here is not novel for readers of the *Année Sociologique* (cf. vol. IV, p. 192 and vol. VI, pp. 363–4); note that it does not exclude an animistic interpretation; since the soul, with the dispositions attributed to it by common opinion during the time following its departure from the body, would naturally appear as the jealous guardian of the taboos imposed on the survivors by mourning, and as the personification of the evil forces which by the fact of death accumulate in the corpse.

[57] Hardeland 1858: 218.

[58] Hickson 1889: 194; Low, in Roth 1896, 1: 155. We confine ourselves here to recalling well-known facts.

[59] Cf., for the Kayan of central Borneo, Nieuwenhuis (1907, 1: 388, 91); for the Olo Ngaju, Grabowsky (1889: 182); Hardeland (1859: 485, 401, 608): the word *rutas* denotes especially funereal impurity, being applied to houses, rivers, and contaminated persons, as well as to the corpse itself; *pali* (= forbidden, causing misfortune) is a general term which corresponds exactly to taboo.

[60] See the references cited in the preceding footnote, and (on the Ot Danom) Schwaner (1854: 76); (on the natives of Luang-Sermata) Riedel (1886: 328–9). Cf. the completely analogous facts reported by Tromp (1888: 71) concerning the Bahau of the upper Mahakam: the victims of a fire are segregated all together outside the village; they are considered possessed by evil spirits; as for those who have not been driven away, the former are forbidden on pain of death to come into contact with them; they may not even receive visits or accept help.

[61] Hardeland 1859: 608; Perelaer 1870: 227.

[62] Hardeland 1859: 36; Nieuwenhuis 1907: 144; Tromp 1877: 47; Roth 1896, 1: 155, 258; 2: 142.—The prohibition is general, but the positive prescriptions vary greatly; so that in Borneo we find three different rules for mourning-garments: a return to the old bark-cloth (Bahau), worn and ragged clothes (Sea Dayak), clothes of one colour, first white then black (Olo Ngaju).

[63] There is no question of giving a complete account here, still less a theory, of mourning among Indonesian peoples: we are concerned only with secondary motifs which play a part in the positive determination of the diverse practices.

[64] At least three, but generally seven (Hardeland 1859: 485).

[65] Grabowsky 1889: 182; or, if they remain in mourning beyond this period, it is to satisfy a personal inclination, not out of duty.

[66] The survivor of two spouses, the parents for their children, and, reciprocally, brothers and sisters (Hardeland 1859: 608); cf., for the Olo Maanyan, Tromp 1877: 47.—It seems that fairly often a single person assumes the responsibility and constraints of mourning; by strict observance, he or she gives dispensation to the others.

[67] Hardeland 1859: 608, 36; cf., for the Dayak of Sarawak, Roth (1896, 1: 130, 156); the widow is thought to belong to her husband until the *gawai antu* (a feast corresponding to the *tivah* among the Olo Ngaju); if she does not remain chaste during this period it is veritable adultery, which is punished as though the husband were still alive. As Grabowsky remarks (1889: 183), this consideration must play a part in the haste with which the death-feast is sometimes held.

[68] The very severity of the mourning-taboos in certain cases prevents the survivors from actively preparing the feast which is to release them; so that there would be no way out of their position if there were not some compromise. The natives of Luang Sermata (cf. Riedel 1886: 328–9) furnish us with a curious example: about two months after the death the relatives of the deceased, after a sacrifice, call a priest in order to learn whether the deceased allows them to leave the village (where they are confined) so that they may collect the things that are needed for the funeral feast; if authorisation is refused, the same attempt is repeated four or six months later; when the deceased has given his consent mourning is at an end and preparations can be made for the final ceremony, which will take place a year or two later.

[69] 1886: 254 ff.—Wilken has brought out well the fact that for the Indonesians 'originally' the end of mourning coincides with the last obsequies and the feast connected with them.

[70] Tromp 1877: 47.

[71] Cf. for example, for the Zambales of the Philippines, Blumentritt (1882: 156); for the Toumbuluh, Riedel (1895: 107).

[72] Grabowsky 1889: 191; Roth 1896, 2: 142, 164 n.

[73] Roth 1896, 1: 155, 210. This fact is to be related to the completely parallel information that we have reported above (p. 35) concerning

the condition of the soul; other authors simply say that the taking of a head has the effect of removing the taboo.

[74] This often happens, as we shall see.

[75] As certain ethnographers mistakenly believe: thus Brinton (1886: 254, 260) considers the practice of secondary burial and the beliefs governing it as the exclusive property of the American race.

[76] Cf. Preuss 1894: 307.

[77] Spencer & Gillen 1904: 506, 517; W. E. Roth 1897: 166.

[78] Krieger 1899: 177–9; Maclay 1875: 301–2; for the Melanesians, Codrington (1891: 261, 268, 288); for the Naga, Godden (1897: 194 ff.).—The Tahitians have retained the memory of a rude epoch when the survivors kept the bodies of the dead in their houses; it is only later, owing to advance in custom, that the practice of erecting special houses for the dead has established itself (Ellis 1839, 1: 404). In our opinion there is no reason to suspect the authenticity of this tradition, and the evolution described in it is probably typical.

[79] Cf., for the Bakundu, Seidel (1896: 277); for the Apingi, du Chaillu (1863: 512); for the Wapare, Baumann (1891: 238).

[80] Cf., for Tahiti, Ellis (1839, 1: 404), Cook in Hawkesworth (1773, 2: 235); for the Gambiers, Moerenhout (1837, 1: 101–2), Cuzent (1872: 78).

[81] Cf. Yarrow 1881: 158, 168 ff.; Schoolcraft 1856, 4: 65; Keating 1824, 1: 345; Catlin 1842, 1: 87 ff.; Adair 1775: 129.

[82] Cf. Simons 1885: 792; Candelier 1893: 216 ff.; and the statements cited by Preuss 1894: 126 ff.

[83] Cf. Swan 1857: 70–1; Yarrow 1881: 166; Preuss 1894: 186. Among the Egyptians mummification seems at first to have been spontaneous; the artificial procedures have been introduced later (Maspero 1892, 1: 112, 116).

[84] Similarly, on Timor a mother has to stay immobile by a continuous fire for four months after the confinement; the heat and the smoke are thought to recondition the body (Müller 1839–44: 275).

[85] The Kurnai sometimes take out the intestines so that desiccation shall take place more quickly (Howitt 1904: 459); this is one of the preliminary operations of embalmment. On certain Melanesian islands the decay of the flesh is accelerated by pouring water over the corpse (Danks 1892: 354; Codrington 1891: 263).

[86] Cf. Howitt on the Unghi of Queensland (1904: 467); on the Papuans, Müller (1839–44: 72), Goudswaard (1863: 71 ff.), Finsch (1885: 86); on the Nigerians, Bosman (1705: 229 ff.), Roth (1903: 42); on the Fjort, Dennett (1898: 22); on the Malagasy, Guillain (1845: 158), Grandidier (1886: 214, 222); for facts from America, Preuss (1894: 187).

[87] As was practised in Tahiti (Hawkesworth 1773: 235; Ellis 1839: 400, 404; Cuzent 1872: 78; Turner 1884: 145, 148); cf. on the Waganda, Declé (1898: 446); on the Antankarana, Grandidier (1886: 217); on the Ainu of Sakhalin, Preuss (1894: 190); the widow of a chief had to protect

his body from putrefaction for a year, until the burial, on pain of being put to death.

[88] Nothing, we believe, proves that this desire is 'natural' and original. Furthermore, most of the accounts cited present mummification as an exceptional rite, reserved for example for chiefs or specially loved children.—The homology between artificial preservation of the corpse and simple temporary exposure may seem less difficult to admit if account is taken of a fact to be adduced below: the dry bones, the residue of decomposition, constitute an incorruptible body for the deceased, exactly as does the mummy.

[89] Maspero 1875: 178; 1892: 292 ff., 358 ff.; cf. *Book of the Dead*, ch. 154; Herodotus, II, 86; Genesis, 50, 3.

[90] We wish to speak here only of cremation practised on the body before (or while) it decomposes; we leave aside the cremation of the bones which sometimes takes place at the final obsequies; cf. p. 54.

[91] Cf. Oldenberg 1903: 494 ff.; Caland 1896: 99 ff. The latter author himself points out (p. 180) the parallel between the erection of the funeral monument and the final obsequies of the Dayak. The rite, moreover, in this complete form is reserved for heads of households who have lit the three fires of the great sacrifices (128); as for others, their remains are simply buried or put into a river (107); but there is only a difference of degree and solemnity between the two ceremonies. Different sources give varying and inexact information on the length of the delay which has to be set between the cremation and the final ceremony (99, 116, 130): the most widespread practice today is to recover the remains on the third day; but the most ancient ceremony seems to make this rite coincide with the end of the ten-day period of impurity.—Among the ancient Aztecs the bones were enclosed in a sort of statue bearing a mask of the deceased; this was kept and honoured for four years; then a second cremation took place, after which the remains of the deceased were buried; this final rite was believed to coincide with the admission of the soul to its last abode (Sahagun 1880: 221; Seler 1902–15, 2: 678, 746; Nuttall 1902: 25 ff., 81 ff.).—Among the Tolkotin of Oregon the calcified bones are returned to the widow, who must carry them about with her for the whole period of her mourning (about three weeks); the release of the widow from this obligation takes place at the time when the bones are placed in the funerary monument (Ross Cox in Yarrow 1881: 144 ff.); similarly among the Takhali (Hale 1846: 203); cf., on the Rucuyen, Crevaux (1882: 120–1).

[92] This homology is still more clear among the Toda; for these expressly call the cremation of the corpse 'the first obsequies', to distinguish this from 'the second obsequies', held at the end of a more or less long period, which consist in a new cremation of the remains and in the final burial of the ashes. During the interval separating the two ceremonies the remains, wrapped in a cloak, are treated as the corpse itself (they are both called by the same name); the soul cannot yet

present itself in the land of the dead and is held to be malevolent, the close relatives are impure and taboo. The intermediary period lasts at least a month, sometimes more than a year. As can be seen, these beliefs and practices agree precisely with the normal type (Rivers 1906: 337, 364 ff., 378 ff., 403, 697, 701).

[93] As is the case, for example, among the Tlinkit (Krause 1885: 222 ff., 227).

[94] In the Australian tribes of the Marlborough region we find cremation practised side by side with provisional burial and with exposure on a platform; it is put on a level with these other modes of disposal (Howitt 1904: 470).

[95] This preoccupation appears explicitly in the incantations uttered to Agni during Hindu cremation: 'Do not destroy him [the deceased], do not harm him; do not shatter his limbs; when thou hast cooked him properly mayst thou send him to our forefathers.' A substitute is also offered to the destructive forces of the fire: the goat which is tethered to the pyre and which is allowed to escape (Caland 1896: 59, 62, 67, 175 ff.). Doubtless there are many adventitious elements, in particular the idea of Agni as psychopomp; but it seems arbitrary to us to restrict (as does Oldenberg [1903: 499]) 'the primitive rôle of the fire' to that of ridding the living of the impure and dangerous object, the corpse; as far back as we may go in the past, the purifying action of cremation, as of the funerary ritual in general, acts for the good of both the survivors and the deceased.—Cf., on the Californian tribes, Powers (1876: 194, 207): the soul can only be saved and liberated by the action of the fire.

[96] Cremation may even be combined with mummification, which seems to be directly opposed to it; thus 'the Quichés used to gather the ashes and solidify them, with the aid of gum, into a statue on which they put a mask representing the features of the deceased; the statue was placed in the grave' (Brasseur de Bourbourg 1861: 192–3).

[97] Cf. Rohde 1898, 1: 30–2.

[98] In Hindu ritual the fire used in cremation (and which must be completely extinguished) is known by the name of *Kravyād*, 'eater of flesh' (Caland 1896: 113).

[99] There are also intermediary forms between simple exposure and complete cremation: the exposure lasts only a few days; as soon as possible the bones are stripped of the burnt flesh; here we have a veritable partial cremation, whose object is to complete more rapidly the desiccation of the bones and the elimination of the impure parts. Cf., on the Santee of South Carolina, Lawson in Mooney (1894: 79); on the Hawaiians, Ellis (1839: 132 ff., 359); Preuss (1894: 309–10). Some authors report the fact that cremation takes place only after a long delay, when decomposition is already well advanced. Cf., on the Tlinkit, Krause (1885: 222, 234) and Erman (1870: 380 ff.); and, on certain Galibi, Biet (1664: 392); note that in the two cases cited cremation follows exposure of the corpse in the house itself.—We do not

maintain that cremation has everywhere succeeded provisional burial or exposure; this would uselessly complicate our thesis with an historical hypothesis which it is impossible to verify; we merely seek to establish that there is an equivalence between these different practices, and that they have to do with the same fundamental preoccupation. The idea that cremation merely reproduces and accelerates the natural process of decomposition has been advanced, in a rather different manner, by Kleinpaul (1898: 93–5).

[100] Cf. Steinmetz 1896.

[101] The nature of these groups varies, however, in the different tribes (Spencer & Gillen 1904: 548; Howitt 1904: 446–9).

[102] This intention appears most clearly in certain cases of infanticide followed by consumption of the flesh by an elder brother or sister whom it is wished to strengthen in this way (Howitt 1904: 749–50; Spencer & Gillen 1904: 608). Howitt reports the widespread belief in the magical properties of human fat: in this resides the strength and health of the individual; in some tribes, the Dieri for example, only the fat is eaten (Howitt 1904: 367, 411, 448).—We do not maintain, however, that this interpretation is exhaustive: thus, among the same Dieri, the consumption of the fat of the deceased is to pacify the relatives and unburden them of their grief; it is still a favourable change brought about in the condition of the survivors.

[103] The Turrbal justify this custom by alleging their affection for the deceased: 'this way they knew where he was, and his flesh would not stink' (Howitt 1904: 752). Cf., on the South American Indians, Preuss (1894: 218): a Masuruna convert complained that in Christian burial he would be eaten by worms instead of by his relatives.

[104] We follow the account of the facts relating to the Binbinga (Spencer & Gillen 1904: 549–54). The bones, wrapped in bark, are first kept some time on a platform until they are completely dry; then they are rewrapped and placed on top of a forked post, sometimes in the very middle of the camp; they stay there for a year or more. The comparison, suggested by the authors themselves, between this series of rites and that found in the neighbouring Gnanji tribe (Spencer & Gillen 1904: 543), is very instructive: among the latter endocannibalism seems to be practised only exceptionally; the corpse is first exposed on a platform in a tree, until the greater part of the flesh has disappeared from the bones; these are then wrapped in bark and left on the platform until they are dry enough to be easily disjointed; then they are put in another wrapping and left in the tree until they are whitened; only then does the final ceremony take place. It can be seen that there is a rigorous correspondence between the two series; the first period of exposure among the Gnanji simply takes the place of the eating of the flesh by the relatives. So we pass easily from the state of affairs observed among the coastal tribes to that which exists in the centre of Australia, for example among the Kaitish, whose final obsequies take place at the end of an exposure of several months in a tree, when all the flesh

has disappeared from the bones (Spencer & Gillen 1904: 508; cf. Howitt 1904: 470, 753). Cf., on the Botocudo, Preuss (1894: 219); on the Chirihuana, Vega (1688: 278).

[105] This is the explanation proposed by Grandidier (1886: 214) concerning the Malagasy: 'This custom seems to have as end that the bones shall not be finally buried with the putrescent matters produced by decomposition and which they consider impure.'

[106] Darmesteter 1892–3, 2: x, 146 ff.

[107] *Vendidad* III, 8 ff.; VII, 25 ff.

[108] These are the famous 'towers of silence' or *dakhma* (Darmesteter 1892–3, 2: 155).

[109] *Vendidad* VI, 44 ff., VIII, 10. It is essential that the corpse 'see the sun' (III, 8 n. 14; VII, 45).

[110] *Vendidad* VII, 46.

[111] *Vendidad* VIII, 33 ff. This declaration is followed by the enunciation of the general principle that 'dry does not mix with dry'.

[112] *Vendidad* VI, 49 ff. and the notes. The custom of secondary burial has fallen into disuse; among contemporary Parsis 'the dried skeletons are thrown twice a year' into the central well of the *dakhma* (Darmesteter 1892–3, 2: 156). But in the ancient custom, still observed in the ninth century, the *dakhma* was a kind of lazaret from which the remains of the dead, once purified, had to be removed. Comparison of Iranian and Hindu rites will be found to confirm the interpretations of cremation that we have given.

[113] Biet 1664: 392; at the end of this period final obsequies are held, to which we shall return. Cf. W. E. Roth (1897: 165) concerning the Bulia tribe in Queensland: 'The savage thinks vaguely of the corpse "becoming older and going away somewhere else", when he stops bringing food and tobacco to the burial place.' Among the Christianised natives of the Paumotu islands the widow and relatives of the deceased come to the grave to watch over him every night, and doubtless bring him food; this rite is obligatory for two weeks, a period corresponding, it is said, to the dissolution of the corpse (Robert Louis Stevenson 1900: 185 ff., 201).

[114] Rath, in Koch (1900: 26); there is no mention in the account of second obsequies.

[115] Cf. Tylor (1876, 1: 558 ff.). On the latter point, see Mariner (1817, 2: 129) on the Fijians; *Geological Survey* 1895: 55 L (on the Eskimo of Labrador): the spirits of material objects are thought to be liberated as soon as the objects disintegrate. In the Irish story reported by Mooney (1888: 295) a son, for the sake of his dead father, orders some clothes and wears them himself: as they wear out, so they go to clothe the father in the other world.

[116] Batchelor (1892: 561). The same idea exists concerning material objects. The author makes no mention of provisional burial, but on the Ainu of Sakhalin see Preuss (1894: 114, 190). Fison found a similar belief in Australia (1881; 140 ff.).

[117] Swan, on the Makah (1870: 84, and cf. 78, 83, 86); Eells, on the Clallam and Twana, in Yarrow (1881: 171, 176); these latter tribes expose the corpse in a raised canoe; final burial takes place about nine months later; among the Makah, at present, the corpse is buried immediately after the death, but there remain, it appears, fairly clear traces of the old custom.

[118] Codrington (1891: 260, cf. 257, 277, 286); the author relates to the same conceptions the practices followed on the island of Saa (with respect to distinguished dead persons), which are intended to accelerate decomposition or to prevent emanations from the body: in this way, souls rich in *mana* will be active and available more quickly, only these becoming *tindalo* (Codrington 1891: 253; Penny 1881: 56). The idea of a temporary sojourn of the soul on earth is also found (Codrington 1891: 267, 284; Penny 1881: 55). Cf. *Reports . . .* 1904, 5: 355.

[119] Codrington 1891: 179–80; Penny 1887: 56.

[120] Lord 1883: 95.

[121] Richardson, on the Betsileo (1875: 73); Shaw (1878: 6–7); Sibree (1880: 277); Grandidier (1886: 221, 225, 231, 217); Guillain (1845: 158). In the case of a prominent person, among the Betsileo, a snake is looked for on the grave after several months and is conducted with ceremony into the town, of which it is henceforth the guardian.— Cf. Hollis (1905: 307): in the case of a rich person or a medicine-man the soul passes into a snake as soon as the corpse putrefies; the snake repairs to the kraal of its children and watches over them.

[122] This assertion is made by Kleinpaul (1898: 31–4); 'What is essential is that the dead should evaporate; for primitives, decomposition is a sort of sublimation, whose products constitute a superior being.'

[123] Cf. note 113 above and Grandidier (1914: 225); Candelier (1893: 218) on the Goajire; close relatives light fires and place food on the grave for nine days, ' for in their eyes one is not really dead until after nine days'; note that this period does not coincide with the duration of the provisional burial, which is one or two years (until the complete desiccation of the bones); cf. Simons 1885: 792.—Cf. Ellis 1839, 1: 404; Riedel 1886: 267 ff. (on the natives of the Aru islands).

[124] See Wilken (1886, Appendix). The soul of the deceased is often believed to follow the widow constantly, keeping an eye on her conduct.— Note that even in societies practising the levirate the new marriage often does not take place until the time of the final ceremony; sometimes, however (among the Chippeway, for example [Yarrow 1881: 184]), it can be concluded earlier, thus relieving the widow of her mourning or dispensing her of it altogether; in this case there is no succession, properly speaking, but a continuation of the deceased by his brother or cousin (Caland 1896: 42).—Accounts concerning these facts are numerous and well known; we cite only a few of them: Spencer & Gillen (1899: 502; 1904: 507); on the natives of the Aru islands, Riedel (1886: 268); on the Papuans, van Hasselt (1891: 10), Rosenberg (1878: 434); on the Maori, Taylor (1870: 99); on the Gilbert Islanders,

Meinicke (1876, 2: 339); on the Iroquois, Lafitau (1724, 2: 439); on the Tolkotin, Yarrow (1881: 145); on the tribes of Guiana, Koch (1900: 70–71); on the Nigerians, Kingsley (1897: 483), Dieterle (1883: 756); on the Fjort, Dennet (1898: 24, 114, 156); on the Ba-Ronga, Junod (1898: 66); on the Malagasy, Grandidier (1886: 217, 226), Rabe (1877: 65). Nothing proves, as Wilken acknowledges, that ritual murder was originally the general rule.

[125] This is the case, for example, among the Ba-Ronga (Junod 1898: 56, 67), the Senga of the Portuguese Zambesi (Declé 1898: 234); cf., on the Barabra, Ruete(1899 : 339).

[126] The Indians of Costa Rica (Gabb 1875: 507; Bovallius 1889: 78); Fjort (Dennett 1898: 178 and *Notes:* 24); the Ba-Ronga (Junod 1898: 56, 128); the Wanyamwesi (Stuhlmann 1894: 90-1); Tongans (Baessler 1895: 332-4).—The same phenomenon is found in another form among the Nigerian tribes of Liberia: the corpse of a king is only finally buried when his successor dies; during the entire reign of the latter, which coincides with the duration of the provisional burial, the ex-king, 'who is not considered to be really dead', watches over his successor and helps him in his functions. Thus a king is truly holder of his office only in the period between his death and that of his successor; in his lifetime he merely exercises a sort of *de facto* regency (Büttikofer 1888: 34, 83-4)— Traces of the same custom are found among the Benin: the accession of the new king can only take place when the death of the former king is accomplished; to make certain of this, the servants who were buried alive with him are questioned; as long as they reply that 'the king is very ill' food is brought and the town is in mourning; when there is silence, towards the fourth or fifth day, the successor is enthroned (Roth 1903: 43; cf. Nassau 1904: 220–1).

[127] The existence of a period of anarchy or a sort of saturnalia, after the deaths of chiefs or their relatives, is a regular phenomenon in certain societies. In Fiji the subject tribes invade the capital and commit every excess without meeting any resistance (Fison 1880: 140); as also in the Carolines (Kubary 1886: 7, 1885a: 70 n. 1) and among the Maori (Colenso 1881 : 59, 63; Dumont d'Urville 1859: 448): the family of the dead chief is despoiled of foodstuffs and movable goods; note that the same reaction follows every violation of a taboo; the death of a chief is a veritable sacrilege, for which his entourage must bear the punishment; the robberies committed by strangers are a necessary expiation.— In the Sandwich Isles the people are prey to a fury which goes by a special name; nearly all actions normally considered criminal are then committed (arson, robbery, murder, etc.), and the women have to prostitute themselves publicly (Ellis 1839, 4: 177, 181; Campbell 1816: 143); cf., on the Mariana Islands, Le Gobien (1700: 68) and on the Gambier Islands, Cuzent (1872: 118); on the Betsileo, Shaw (1878: 6-7); on the Tschi, Dieterle (1883: 757); on the Waidah, Bosman (1705: 390 ff.): 'As soon as the king's death is public, everybody steals from his neighbour as best he can . . . without anyone having the

I

right to punish, as if justice died with the king.' The thefts cease as soon as the successor is proclaimed.

[128] See the preceding note; cf. Grandidier 1886: 218, 220.

[129] Fison 1881: 141: the author makes no mention of double burial. Williams (1858: 187) merely says that at Vanua Levu the announcement of the death of a chief is the signal for pillage; there is no question of keeping the death secret for a time. The same author reports (204) an interesting tradition which seems to attest the former existence of a rite of exhumation (cf. 198).

[130] Thus on Tahiti a ceremony which takes place immediately after the corpse is placed on the platform is meant to 'bury the impurity' so that it shall not affect the survivors (Ellis 1839: 401–3).—Cf., on the Maori, Taylor (1870: 99). Similarly, Avestan ritual prescribes that a 'four-eyed yellow dog' shall be led to the corpse; the look of this dog 'strikes the infection'; it is explicitly said that this rite of Sagdîd reduces, but does not suppress, the danger of impurity (Darmesteter 1892: xi, 149; *Vendidad* VII, 29; VIII, 16 ff.).

[131] It has a special name in Tahiti: *aumiha* (Ellis 1839: 405).—Among the Bribri of Costa Rica the most impure thing (after the body of a woman pregnant for the first time) is a corpse; an animal which passes near the temporary resting-place is defiled and must be killed; its flesh may not be eaten (Gabb 1875: 499).—Similarly, the *dakhma* are cursed places 'where bands of demons swoop down, where illnesses are produced', where crimes are perpetrated (*Vendidad* VII, 56).

[132] Man (1882: 281; 1883: 141); garlands of leaves are hung around an abandoned village to warn strangers of the peril.

[133] Verguet 1885: 193; Somerville 1899: 404.

[134] We understand by this word, not the violent emotional crisis which occurs directly after the death, sometimes after the death-throes, but the durable and prolonged condition imposed on certain relatives of the deceased for a set period. On this distinction (which is not at all absolute) see Ellis (1839: 407), Lafitau (1724; 2: 438), Nassau (1904: 219).

[135] Among the Toda, the word *kedr*, meaning 'corpse', means at the same time the interval between the first and second obsequies and the special condition in which the relatives of the deceased are during this period (Rivers 1906: 368).

[136] Shortland (1882: 52). The account adds that before the expiry of the fixed period the son transgresses one of the prohibitions; 'then the sacred remains of his father turned against him, and he died.' We should notice in passing that here the soul of the deceased is believed to pass the period of transition in the dark land of the dead under the earth: perhaps there is a connection between this belief and the fact that the mode of provisional sepulture practised is burial; the final destiny of the souls of chiefs is to go to rejoin the gods in the sky (Taylor 1870: 100). There is certainly no need to see the arbitrary fantasy of a dying person in the account referred to; for the prescribed rites are really observed, with

the reservation that the delay before the exhumation is in general only two years (Taylor 1870: 99; Tregear 1889: 105).—Note, however, that among the same Maori the closest relative of the deceased can, by appropriate rites, be freed of the special quality that he has contracted, and the tie uniting him to the deceased can be broken; the period of mourning is then extremely reduced (Shortland 1882: 53–63).

[137] We have offered the conjecture that where the duration of mourning does not coincide with that of provisional burial there has been a reduction: see above, p. 39. This fact seems historically demonstrable, so far as Fiji is concerned. On this island (where the first obsequies are definitive) mourning last only ten to twenty days; now this period is called 'the hundred nights', which is precisely the duration of mourning and of provisional burial on other Melanesian islands. It seems therefore that Fijian mourning, which originally lasted a hundred days, has undergone a reduction. Cf. Wilken 1887: 349; Codrington 1891: 282–4; Somerville 1897: 403–4.

[138] Cf., on the Australians, Spencer & Gillen (1904: 530), Howitt (1904: 459, 467–8, 471); on the Papuans of New Guinea, Turner (1884: 348), van Hasselt (1886: 118); on the Tud Islanders, Gill (Reports . . . 1904: 258); on the Aru Islanders, Kolff (1840: 167), Riedel (1886: 267), Ribbe (1888: 191), Webster (1898: 209); on the natives of New Britain, the Banks Islands, and the Gilberts, Danks (1892: 354), Codrington (1891: 268), Hale (1846: 99–100), Meinicke (1876: 339); on the Malagasy, Grandidier (1886: 217). Among the Tolkotin of Oregon the same rite is observed by the widow at the time of the cremation (Cox, in Yarrow 1881: 144 ff.).

[139] Spencer & Gillen 1904: 530; van Hasselt 1886: 118.

[140] These practices are thus sometimes confused with endocannibalism properly speaking.

[141] It is commonly the case that a tabooed object conceals a magical power capable of being used under certain conditions; the rite in question here may thus become a simple magical operation, having no longer any connection with mourning (Kingsley 1897: 478; dos Santos, in Theal 1897, 7: 289).

[142] Similarly, embalmers on Tahiti were avoided by everybody for as long as they were at work, for the mortuary impurity attached to them; they could not feed themselves, for fear that the food, defiled by the contact of their hands, should cause their death (Ellis 1839: 403).

[143] Cf. Junod 1898: 55, 471; Casalis 1859: 269.

[144] Goddard 1903, 1: 78; 2: 35; people in mourning are placed, with recently confined or menstruating women, in the category of persons with a 'bad body', spoiled.—Among the Unalit of Alaska, on the first day after death, all the inhabitants of the village consider themselves soft and nerveless; they have only a feeble power of resistance to malign influences; the next day they declare themselves to be a little harder; the third day they say that as the corpse is in the course of freezing they approach a return to their normal solidity; a bath of urine then

delivers them from the evil and resolidifies their flesh (Nelson 1899: 313 ff.). We see that there is a close connection between the state of the corpse and that of the survivors. Should we see this idea as a particular form (related to the arctic climate) of the general belief concerning the dissolution of the body? Note that the soul does not leave the earth until the fourth day after death, and that, at least among the Eskimo of the lower Yukon (Kwikpagemut), the obsequies do not take place until after the same lapse of time (Jacobsen 1884:196; see below, p. 52).

[145] This is the name by which people in mourning are called on the island of Mabuiag (*Reports* . . . 5, 1904: 249).

[146] Among the Basuto the same word signifies darkness and mourning (Casalis 1859: 335).

[147] We cite as example the series of mourning-taboos found among the Kwakiutl: for four days the closest relative of the deceased must not make a movement; then, after a ceremony of ablution, he may move a little but not walk for twelve days; if he is spoken to, this is sure to cause the death of a relative; he is fed twice a day by an old woman, at low tide, with salmon caught the year before (note that all these elements belong to the order of things contrary to life); by stages, he progressively regains the liberty to move and to speak to others (Boas 1887: 427). An absolute silence is even imposed on different groups of female relatives of the deceased during the whole mourning-period among the Warramunga (Spencer & Gillen 1904: 525). A typical form of food-taboo is found among the natives of one of the islands of the New Hebrides: 'good food' is forbidden to the immediate relatives of the deceased; notably, they may not eat the fruit of cultivated trees, but only wild fruits from the forest (Codrington 1891: 281). Finally, we should remember the common fact that people in mourning are 'dispensed of the duties of courtesy', must abstain in general from social labour, public feasts and assemblies, and ceremonies of worship (Lafitau 1724, 2: 438).

[148] Cf., on the Köggaba Indians of Colombia, Sievers (1886: 97); on the Colorado of Equador, Seler (1902: 6); on the Saccha, Koch (1900: 85).

[149] These ideas also enter in the case of double burial, determining the period judged necessary to complete the desiccation; so that the final ceremony often coincides with the anniversary of the death.

[150] Cf., on the Eskimo, Nelson (1899: 310 ff., 319, 427); L. Turner (1894: 192–3); Pinart (1873: 5); Venjaminov (1849: 122), etc.; for the Otoe Indians, Yarrow (1881: 97); the Hidatsa Sioux, Yarrow (1881: 199); for the Zuni, Stevenson (1904: 307–8); for the Hopi, Voth (1905: 20); for the Sia, Stevenson (1894: 145); for the Aztec, see above, note 91; for the Pipil, Palacios in Ternaux-Compans (1840: 37); in certain of these accounts the period is not four days but four months or years.—The number 40 plays the same rôle among various peoples; cf., on the Rumanians, Flachs (1899: 63); on the Bulgarians, Strausz (1898: 451–3); on the (Muslim) Abchas of the Caucasus, von Hahn

(1900: 244–6) (the soul is prey to expiatory sufferings, the relatives are in deep mourning); on the Barabra, Muslims of Nubia, Ruete (1899: 339); on the Cheremis, Smirnov (1898, 1: 140–4) (the obligation on the relatives to provide nourishment for the deceased ends with the fortieth day); finally, we may recall the forty days elapsing between the death and the funeral ceremonies of the ancient kings of France, during which period food was served to an effigy representing the deceased (Lalanne 1847: 294).—On the important rôle of the sacred number 3 (or 9) in the funeral customs of the ancient Greeks and Romans, see Diels (1890: 40–1).

[151] The *tivah* of the Olo Ngaju ordinarily lasts for seven days (Grabowsky 1889: 196). On Halmahera the ceremonies last a whole month and sometimes more (van Baarda 1883: 903).

[152] Kloss tells us of the inhabitants of Kar Nicobar that this is the most important of all their ceremonies (1903: 285).

[153] See, on Timor, Forbes (1885: 434); Braches (1882: 105) cites the case of Dayak who engage themselves as slaves in order to be able to meet the expenses of the *tivah*; this feast, according to Schwaner (Roth 1896, 2: clxxiii) is the most costly in the Barito basin.

[154] Among the Topebato of central Celebes, at a feast not thought to be very important, 80 buffaloes, 20 goats, and 30 pigs are put to death (Kruyt 1895: 35). Rosenberg (1878: 27) mentions the figure of 200 buffaloes (in the case of a chief) for the Batak of Pertibi.

[155] Cf. Perham on the Sea Dayak (Roth 1896, 1: 207); Grabowsky on the Olo Maanyan (1884: 472). On Kar Nicobar all the villages of the island are invited to the feast (Solomon 1902: 205). From 800 to 1000 persons sometimes participate in the main feast of the *tivah* (Grabowsky 1889: 203).

[156] Hardeland 1858: 351; Grabowsky 1889: 188.

[157] Cf., on the Olo Maanyan, Grabowsky (1884: 47) and Tromp (1877: 47); for the Alfuru of central Celebes, Kruyt (1895: 34): the interval averages about three years; among the Toundae the rule is to hold the feast when there have been ten deaths in the village; its date is never rigorously fixed.—For the inhabitants of Kar Nicobar, Kloss (1903: 285 ff.) and Solomon (1902: 209): the feast is held every three or four years, but not all the inhabitants of the island can celebrate it at the same time (doubtless because the different villages act as helpers and guests to each other). Also they wait until the remains of all the dead are dried up.—Elsewhere this last condition is not observed; it follows that the date of the final obsequies is independent of the state of the corpse.

[158] About thirty on the average, in the case of the *sandong raung* (Grabowsky 1889: 189): when a *sandong* is full a second is built, then a third beside this (Perelaer 1870: 246).

[159] Hardeland 1859: 503; Braches 1882: 101; Grabowsky 1889: 188–9, 200–1; Meyer & Richter 1896: 125 ff.—*Raung* means 'coffin', *tulang* 'bones'. Often the *sandong tulang* is mounted on only one post.—

The custom of cremating the bones is found among different peoples of the Malay Archipelago, e.g. the Batak (Hagen 1883: 517), the Balinese (Crawfurd 1820: 255; van Eck in Wilken 1884: 52); the Ot Danom (Schwaner 1854: 76, 151). This custom is perhaps due to Hindu influence; in any case, it does not alter the normal Indonesian type in any way.

[160] Cf. Schwaner 1853: 217–18; 1854: 7, 85, 120; Grabowsky 1884: 47; Müller 1839–44: 402: a village prided itself on the number of *sandong* it contained, because of the wealth they represented.

[161] This removal to a distance probably has to do with the *pali* or taboo on the ossuary (Braches 1882: 103; Grabowsky 1889: 198 n. 1).—The accounts of the Olo Ngaju do not permit us to be certain whether all the *sandong* of the different families composing the village are found together in such a way as to constitute a cemetery; such as is certainly the case, according to Tromp (1877: 43) and Grabowsky (1884: 474), among the Olo Maanyan of the Sihong.

[162] Thus the *salong* of the Kayan corresponds to the *sandong raung*, and the Sea Dayak *klirieng* to the *sandong tulang* (Roth 1896, 1: 146, 148; Nieuwenhuis 1907, 1: 90); and, for Halmahera, van Baarda (1883: 903).

[163] Cf. Roth 1896, 1: 146, 152, 153; Grabowsky 1888: 583; Kükenthal 1896–1902: 270; Tromp 1888: 92; Schwaner, in Roth 1896, 2: cxcvii; this last author notes the possibility of this connection. The accounts cited seem to furnish the intermediaries between the living tree of the Orang Ot and the *sandong tulang*.

[164] Cf., for Borneo, Grabowsky (1889: 200), Nieuwenhuis (1907, 1: 376), Tromp (1888: 76), Creagh (1897: 33)—description of a cave containing forty coffins; for Celebes, Riedel (1895: 108–9), Meyer and Richter (1896: 139), Adriani (1899: 28, 38), Kruyt (1895: 236), Matthes (1865: 68–9); the last author visited three large underground caverns; each one of them contained a mass of bones of dead people, one ranged by the other, a large number being enclosed in coffins; these caverns had been used as regular burial places before the introduction of Islam.

[165] We have not exhausted the list: thus (final) burial is sometimes mentioned.

[166] Braches (1882: 101).—On the island of Nias, during an analogous ceremony to which we shall return, the widow calls the deceased and says to him: 'We have come to seek you, to take you away from your lonely hut and lead you to the great mansion (of the ancestors)' (Chatelin 1880: 149); (the lonely hut is identical with the *pasah* of the Olo Ngaju; see above, note 10).—We believe that the expressions in the song opening the *tivah* should be interpreted in the same sense: the spirits are begged to come 'to put an end to the wandering state of the deceased, . . . like a bird lost in the air . . . like a golden grain of sand carried away in the stream . . .' etc. (Hardeland 1858: 219).

[167] Grabowsky 1889: 191; Tromp 1877: 47; Kruyt 1895: 32: when the corpse has been kept in the house of the living it is also removed to the *balai* (Grabowsky 1884: 472).

[168] Grabowsky 1889: 192; Kruyt 1895: 230.

[169] Kruyt 1895: 26.

[170] Cf., for the Olo Lowangan, Grabowsky (1888: 583); for the Dayak of Kutai, Tromp (1888: 76); for the Murut, Roth (1896, 1: 153); for the Babar Islanders, Riedel (1886: 362); for the Nicobar, Solomon (1902: 209). We have not found this practice expressly mentioned among the Olo Ngaju; we are told only that the remains are transferred to a new coffin (Grabowsky 1889: 200).

[171] Kruyt 1895: 26, 33. It is not only a physically repugnant operation but full of supernatural dangers.

[172] We follow Kruyt (1895: 26, 33, 232): the bones are swaddled in bark from a certain tree. In some districts the head is adorned with a wooden mask during the feast (231); the bones, with their wrappings, are placed in a very small coffin (235).—Cf. for Timor, Forbes (1885: 435).

[173] The Olo Maanyan, who practise cremation of the bones, consider this an indispensable act of purification (Tromp 1877: 48).

[174] A passage by Hardeland (1859: 308 s.v. *liau*) seems to confirm and complete this interpretation: in order that the *liau krahang* or corporeal soul may be reunited with the principal soul, all the remains of the corpse are collected (with prayers to the good spirits to attach to them all the hairs, nails, etc. that the deceased may have lost during his lifetime); then Tempon Telon, the mythical psychopomp, brings forth the *liau krahang* from them, which his wife sprinkles with a life-giving water; the soul, thus returned to life and consciousness, is then conducted to the heavenly city. As, in the whole of this ceremony, the (imaginary) events relative to the soul are the exact counterpart of the things done to the corpse, it seems indubitable to us that the priestesses themselves perform the act they attribute to the wife of Tempon. The object of this rite is a veritable resurrection of the body.

[175] By virtue of the axiom 'Rich here below, rich above' (Braches 1882: 102; Grabowsky 1889: 192-3).—Without doubt the soul of each of these objects is believed to follow the deceased; naturally, the living family exalts itself, in its dead, before the eyes of the strangers present.

[176] Kruyt 1895: 33, 235; this interpretation by the author seems, however, to reduce the significance of the rite; as is indicated by the presence of priestesses and the fact of their chants, it is an action directly concerning the welfare of the dead; the words of the song are very obscure. Perhaps this rite should be likened to that which is described in the following paragraph.

[177] Hardeland 1859: 609; Grabowsky 1889: 200-1; cf. on the Murut, Roth 1896, 1: 153.

[178] Braches 1882: 103: the *sandong*, with everything around it, is *pali*.

[179] Van Lier, on Timor Laut (1901: 216).—One is also forced to remain in contact with the dead: among the Alfuru of central Celebes

small pieces of the bark used to adorn the bones are kept: they are carried in war to assure the protection of the dead (Kruyt 1895: 231 n. 1). Similarly, on the island of Babar, the women charged with putting the remains in a mountain cave bring back tree-branches from there and distribute the leaves to the inhabitants of the village (Riedel 1886: 362).— Certain Alfuru of eastern Celebes go so far as to share out the bones among the members of the family, who attribute magical virtues to them (Bosscher and Matthissen, in Wilken 1884: 179).

[180] The other bones are either taken to a collective ossuary or are not exhumed at all; cf., for the Nicobar, Solomon (1902: 209), Kloss (1903: 82); for the Toba Batak, Wilken (1889: 98); for the Dayak, Grabowsky (1888: 583) on the Olo Lowangan; Bangert, in Wilken (1889: 95–6), on the Olo Maanyan; Tromp (1888: 76) on the Tunjung; for Buru, Forbes (1885: 324): the son of the deceased wears the two first vertebrae of the skeleton in order to avert misfortune from his person.—Note that among certain peoples, who do not keep relics, the heads of the dead only are gathered in a collective resting-place (Riedel 1886: 142, 362).

[181] Cf. the reference cited in footnote 180, and Perham in Roth (1896, 1: 211). In this case it is a matter of a cult of the ancestors, at least of certain ancestors; but though the final ceremony is susceptible of becoming the starting point of a cult in this way, it is not necessarily a form of worship. Indonesian second obsequies are no different in their function from our funeral ceremonies, they are not intended for the adoration or propitiation of deified souls. We should not be deluded by the fact that they are held long after the death: an act of worship is repeated indefinitely at a certain interval, whilst on the contrary the feast for the deceased ends a series of acts.

[182] Cf. note 171.—On Nicobar exhumation is considered a very dangerous operation, calling for special precautions and purifications (Solomon 1902: 209). In the south of the island of Nias this task was imposed on an individual seized by violence, and whose head was then cut off and placed with the remains of the deceased (Donleben 1848: 180). Recent authors, particularly Modigliani (1890: 280) have not observed anything like this: a dead person is buried for good.

[183] As, for example, the Olo Maanyan (Grabowsky 1884: 471). The old custom is only maintained by the people of the Sihong river.

[184] Cf. note 172.

[185] Kruyt 1895: 35.—The rite of destruction of the (temporary) 'house' of the deceased at the final ceremony is also found on the island of Sumba, together with the final closing of the tomb, which till then was only covered by a dried buffalo skin (Roos 1872: 56–8).—Among the Olo Ngaju themselves, sometimes there is no exhumation of the remains; in this case, a finely-carved length of bamboo is planted on the grave, to the recitation of appropriate expressions; this is a sign for the soul that it can enter the town of the dead (Grabowsky 1889: 193); cf. also Riedel (1886: 329) on the natives of Luang Sermata.—In the

gawai antu, the great funeral feast of the Sea Dayak, there are generally no second obsequies; there is simply the erection of an ironwood monument on the grave in certain cases, at the same time as food is brought to it (Roth 1896, 1: 204–5, 208–9, 258).

[186] Cf., on the Olo Ngaju, Grabowsky (1889: 185 ff.): the main ordeal is passing through a whirlwind of fire; on the Bahau of central Borneo, Nieuwenhuis (1907: 104).

[187] This is the most famous of the *sangiang*, or good spirits of the air; he is called, after his principal slave, by the name of 'master of Telon'; but his real name is Rawing, the Crocodile (Hardeland 1858: 352 n. 43). In this connection, it is interesting to note that the carvings which ornament the *sandong* are generally snakes and crocodiles (Perelaer 1870: 246). On the other hand, in a passage of the priestesses' song Tempon Telon declares himself to be a tiger: now the Dayak of the Mahakam give their distinguished dead a wooden tiger with the head of a crocodile, which is doubtless entrusted with helping the soul on its journey (Tromp 1888: 63); and the tiger, associated with a crocodile or snake, is often represented near the *sandong* (Hardeland 1858: 257; Grabowsky 1889: Pl. IX, Fig. 9). The hornbill has an analogous rôle. It is remarkable that these terms—tiger, crocodile, or hornbill—are constantly used in the priestesses' jargon to designate men and women, as well as persons already established in the other world. It is well known that the belief in a special kinship between man and the crocodile or tiger, and in a transmigration of the soul after death into the body of one of these, is frequently met with in the Malay Archipelago (Epp 1841: 159–60; Wilken 1884: 68 ff.); for the hornbill, Pleyte (1885: 313; 1886: 464).

[188] Hardeland 1858: 209; Grabowsky 1884: 197–8.

[189] Hardeland 1858: 236 ff.

[190] Hardeland 1858: 252. For what follows we refer to Ullmann, in Grabowsky (1889: 197–8); for the description of the journey in Hardeland is summary, and in particular makes no mention of ordeals to be passed through.

[191] Evidenced by cries of joy and an infernal din (Grabowsky 1889: 198).

[192] Those whom the deceased had 'sent ahead' during his lifetime, by taking their heads, or victims sacrificed at the feast (Braches 1882: 102–3).

[193] Hardeland 1858: 269–73.—Note the symmetry between these images and the practices observed in the course of the obsequies: the circulation of the souls round the celestial mansion corresponds to the dance of the priestesses round the *sandong* (cf. p. 56), and the adornment of new arrivals at the laying out of the material remains.

[194] Modelled, though, on the preceding (Hardeland 1858: 283).

[195] Everybody lives together; families are recomposed (Grabowsky 1889: 186; cf. Kruyt 1895: 28–9). Certain categories of dead persons, however, live apart: we shall return to this point.

[196] Grabowsky 1889: 187; Kruyt 1895: 28–9.

[197] Grabowsky 1889: 188; but he is wrong to apply to the soul the word used to designate the feast: *tivah*, as we shall see, must be understood to relate to the survivors.

[198] Braches 1882: 102–3. He concludes: 'The *tivah* thus has no other object than to transport the bones of the deceased from the provisional coffin to the *sandong*, and to lead the soul from "the hill where the coffin was hidden" to the place of the *sandong*.'

[199] Grabowsky 1889: 190.—One Dayak, after hearing the sermon of a missionary one day, said: 'Our heaven is the *sandong*' (Grabowsky 1889: 198). This should not be seen as a denial of the heavenly 'town of the souls'; this phrase was meant simply to oppose to the Christian preaching the system of beliefs of which the *sandong* is the visible expression.—Cf. on the Alfuru, Kruyt (1895: 235).

[200] Braches 1882: 105.

[201] Among certain Dayak tribes of Sarawak the number of successive deaths is only three (Roth 1896, 1: 213); Chalmers (in Roth 1896, 1: 167) mentions four, but the first corresponds to the end of the transitory period and to the entry into the land of souls; during each existence the soul bears a distinct name. The same belief in three successive deaths is found among the Alfuru of central Celebes (Kruyt 1895: 29): the soul passes each time into new surroundings; the names of these different places are obviously of Hindu or Muslim origin; but the basis of the belief is original.—The natives of Nias believe in nine successive deaths: the lives of the other world last exactly the same number of years as the preceding earthly existence (Wilken 1884: 61–2).

[202] According to Perelaer (1870: 17–18), the Dayak willingly eat the meat from these animals because since they are exclusively herbivorous there is a very good chance that there may be a human soul in them. To the contrary, Hendrich (1888: 106–7) tells us that many Dayak do not eat the flesh of deer or wild boar, nor the leaves of certain palms, because the souls of their grandparents might be in them. The two reports, contradictory though they are, agree in the essential point. Braches (1882: 103) tells us that according to the Olo Ngaju buffaloes have the same great-grandfather as men; therefore they are sacrificed at the *tivah* instead of the prohibited human beings. Cf. Nieuwenhuis 1907, 1: 103, 106.

[203] We report the belief in the form it takes among the Olo Ngaju (Braches 1882: 102; Grabowsky 1889: 187) and the Olo Maanyan (Grabowsky 1884: 471). But it is found, at least fragmentarily, among other peoples of the Archipelago.—cf., for the Balinese, Wilken (1884: 61–2): after its celestial existence the soul redescends on earth in the form of dew and is reincarnated in a child of the same family, which explains atavistic resemblances; for the island of Nias, Wilken (1884: 65); for the northwestern Dayak, Roth (1896, 1: 167, 213, 217–19); in many tribes the belief in a reincarnation has disappeared: the soul returns to earth as dew or disappears in some unnamed plant or insect of the

forest; its real and personal existence is abolished. This is doubtless an impoverishment of the primitive belief of which the Olo Ngaju may give us an idea.

[204] Cf. Perham in Roth (1896, 1: 208): the presence of the dead is desired, but only at a suitable time and in a suitable way.

[205] See above, pp. 36–7.—Cf. St. John in Roth (1896, 2: 142): 'Then [after the feast] the Dayak forget their dead and the ghosts of the dead forget them.'

[206] The living offer sacrifices to the dead, the dead assure by their power the success of earthly undertakings, particularly the harvest (Kruyt 1895: 31, 36).

[207] On the island of Roti, the same day as the soul departs for the land of the dead, a palm leaf is cut in a particular way and is sprinkled with the blood of a sacrificial animal; this object (called *maik*), which henceforth bears the name of the deceased, is then attached to other identical ones, representing those who died previously, and is hung under the roof; this ceremony, we are told, is equivalent to a canonisation of the deceased. When the *maik* disappears, due to wear and worms, it is not replaced: two classes of spirits (*nitu*) are distinguished, those of within, who still have their *maik* and to whom sacrifices are offered inside the house, and by those without, whose names no longer live in the memory of the living, and to whom sacrifices are made outside. Thus the domestic cult is concerned only with the closest ancestors; after a certain time the souls are lost in the collectivity of souls common to the whole village (Heijmering 1844: 365–6, 91; Graafland 1890: 168; Müller 1839–44: 289; Wilken 1885: 195). Cf., for the Philippines, Blumentritt (1882: 150).—In the north of the island of Nias there exists, besides the shadow-soul which goes to the other world soon after death, a heart-soul which is transformed after twenty or thirty days into a more or less authentic spider; this stays near the corpse until its relatives come to seek it on the grave and take it with great pomp to the family house, where it lives in a tiny statuette attached to images of the ancestors and placed near the hearth (Chatelin 1881: 147–155; Modigliani 1890: 290, 293 ff., 646–7). It appears certain that the ceremony of extracting the souls, celebrated for a number of dead at the same time, is identical with the final funerary feast (after the abandonment of the rite of secondary obsequies).

[208] These facts are closely related to those adduced above, pp.56–7; perhaps the *maik* or the statuette should even be seen as substitutes for the head of the deceased. Certain islands of Timor Laut present us with a transitional form: the head of the deceased is kept in the house, and a statuette representing him is also made. The soul does not reside permanently either in the skull or in the statuette; when it is summoned it is left to choose between these two places: the fact that a fly settles on one or the other reveals the choice of the soul (Wilken 1885: 178–9).

[209] It is this part of the final ceremony that gives it its name among the Olo Ngaju; for the word *tivah* means 'to be free, released from

prohibition'; it is the exact opposite of *pali* (in the same way as *noa* is opposed to *tabu*) (Hardeland 1859: 608).

²¹⁰ Grabowsky 1889: 196.—Perham, in Roth (1896, 1: 209), mentions an analogous rite among the Dayak of Sarawak which, he says, forms an important element of the feast: a certain quantity of *tuak* (intoxicating drink) is set aside in a bamboo and consecrated to the souls; it is solemnly drunk by an old person.

²¹¹ Therefore the relatives of the deceased are often called by this appellation in the song of the priestesses (Hardeland 1858: 216).

²¹² Hardeland 1858: 225 ff., 276.

²¹³ This is the well-known operation in healing magic, which consists in extracting from the body of the patient the harmful thing that was lodged there; here the spirits (and perhaps in fact the priestesses) remove 'the stone that limits [i.e. shortens] life'.

²¹⁴ Hardeland 1858: 246; we have extracted these expressions, by way of example, from a much longer series which is repeated several times (with some variants) in the course of these chants (cf. 216 ff., 231, 244, 323).

²¹⁵ Hardeland 1858: 245: the misfortune is rendered inert, without strength, like fish in a poisoned river.

²¹⁶ Cf. above, p. 55. The same action which gives rebirth into another life, when applied to the remains of the deceased, renews the person of the survivors.

²¹⁷ Hardeland 1858: 276 ff., 290. At the basis of all these accounts there is the distinction between two opposed kinds of magical power: one (*sial, palahan*) comprising everything that diminishes the vital or social power of the individual, the other constituting or reinforcing this same power. The effort of the priestess tends to paralyse the adverse power which seized the relatives of the deceased during the period of mourning, and on the other hand to put at their disposal a large reserve of beneficent (mystical) energy.

²¹⁸ Cf. Hardeland 1858: 231, 354 n. 77.

²¹⁹ This change is even physical: during the mourning-period the bones were disjointed (as is the case, the Dayak say, each time the body is exhausted or weak); at the *tivah* they are joined together again.

²²⁰ The house and furniture also have to be purified: to this end they are scraped and beaten, so as to drive out the 'bad things' (conceived as living persons); these alight on the priestesses, who take them outside and chase them away on boats towards 'their home in the middle of the sea' (Hardeland 1858: 328 ff., 368; Grabowsky 1889: 202).

²²¹ Cf. Wilken 1884: 124; 1886: 258; 1889: 98; St. John in Roth 1896, 2: 143.

²²² Grabowsky 1889: 194, 198 ff.; cf., on the Sea Dayak, Roth (1896, 1: 258): the aspersion of the relatives with the blood of the victim is to 'mark that the *ulit* or taboo is removed'.—Such is the complex and original form of the rite; but when a living prisoner or slave is not available a head is obtained by murder, over which the men perform a

simulated sacrifice (Tromp 1888: 81). When the authors mention simply
'the acquisition of a human head' it means that the report has been
abbreviated or that the rite has undergone a simplification: 'head-
hunting' is a substitute for genuine sacrifice.

²²³ We cannot adduce a positive proof of this last assertion; cf.,
however, Rosenberg (1878: 157 ff.): in southern Nias matters are so
arranged that the victim exhales his last breath on to the corpse (the
feast is held soon after the death). We can only speculate by analogy
that the blood of the victim must have been used to revivify the remains
(cf. above note 174).

²²⁴ It may seem surprising that we do not mention here the belief
which appears prominently in many accounts, and which Wilken,
among others, considers the genesis of funeral sacrifice: the souls of the
victims serve as slaves or keep the deceased company in the heavenly city.
This is because for us this idea, however widespread it may be, is secondary and does not express the nature of the rite. Wilken's interpretation
obliges him to consider funerary sacrifice as a separate kind, radically
distinct from human sacrifice practised on other occasions (birth of a
son, marriage, inauguration of a new house, etc.); whereas fundamentally
all these cases are the same operation: changing the state of persons
or things in order to permit them to enter a new phase of their lives.—Cf.
Hubert & Mauss 1899.

²²⁵ Grabowsky 1889: 203 ff.; 1884: 474, 448–9; 1888: 583–4.—
Among the Olo Ngaju the family of the deceased board a boat which is
capsized by the priestesses in mid-river: this is repeated three times.
Among the Olo Maanyan the participants in the feast are bathed in the
blood of animals sacrificed above their heads in the *balai* itself; in the
course of this ceremony a large wooden statue is erected at the entrance
to the village, which is meant to prolong to the next feast of the same sort
the good effects of that just held, and to keep evil spirits at a distance.

²²⁶ Grabowsky 1889: 202–3; Perham, in Roth 1896, 1: 209; Tromp
1888: 81.

²²⁷ Among the Arunta the totemic ancestors formed a more or less
numerous group, whereas among the Warramunga it is usually a single
ancestor who is thought to have given birth to all the souls currently
available to the group; the difference is not absolute, since even among
the Arunta the ancestors left behind them other souls not their own,
bound to sacred objects (*churinga*) which they carried with them (Spencer
& Gillen 1904: 150 ff., 161 ff.).

²²⁸ This is explicitly stated of the Arunta (Spencer & Gillen 1899:
123 ff.; 1904: 150, ch. xiii *passim*); but in other tribes the death of one
or more ancestors is not given as a necessary condition for the formation
of a totemic centre; individual souls, like animals and plants, issued
from the body of the ancestor when he was performing ceremonies
(Spencer & Gillen 1904: 157, 162, 301); elsewhere the death of the
ancestors has the same effect (Spencer & Gillen 1904: 204, 247, 250);
note that among the Warramunga the colonies of souls which nourish the

group whose totem is the mythical serpent Wollunqua seem to have been formed at the places where the single ancestor tried to penetrate under the earth before he finally succeeded (Spencer & Gillen 1904: 241–2).

[229] Spencer & Gillen 1904: 330–1, 157 n. 1, 313.

[230] Which frequently happens among the Arunta (Spencer & Gillen 1904: 581): this name is sacred and is known to only the oldest members of the totemic group.

[231] Every individual knows exactly from which place the soul incarnated in him comes, and he is united by a close relation to this place, which is sacred to him; his secret name is sometimes derived from it (among the Warramunga); this 'motherland' of his soul forms his identity and determines his position and function in the religious community (Spencer & Gillen 1899: 132; 1904: 448 ff., 583–4, 254, 264).

[232] See above, p. 44.

[233] Spencer & Gillen 1904: 550–4, 173–4.

[234] The author's description refers to certain groups of the southern part of this tribe.

[235] As soon as these have been taken from the temporary resting-place they are placed without ceremony in an ant-hill, which has no external sign to denote their presence (Spencer & Gillen 1904: 532–3). Perhaps this practice should be linked to the fact that ant-hills are sometimes considered the seat of souls left behind by the ancestors: the fact is attested precisely for the totemic group to which belonged the individual whose obsequies the authors saw (Spencer & Gillen 1904: 241).

[236] Similarly, among the Binbinga the radius is set apart; after the final ceremony it is used in the expedition made to avenge the deceased; it is not buried until later, by the side of the coffin containing the other bones (Spencer & Gillen 1904: 554, 463).—It is not only among the Australians that the radius is the object of special representations: thus among the Papuans of Roon (northeast New Guinea), while the other bones are collected in a cave, the radii of different deceased persons are placed in a small house. Note that in the course of this ceremony the men perform a dance imitating a snake; this represents, it is said, the death of an immense snake which, according to legend, formerly desolated the country (van Balen 1886: 567 ff., 571–2).

[237] Spencer & Gillen 1904: 168. We know that among the Warramunga the totemic groups are divided between the two phratries which constitute the tribe: it appears that there is a fairly close solidarity between the different groups composing the same phratry (248, 163).

[238] Cf. Spencer & Gillen 1904: 193 ff.; similarly, the other obsequies that Spencer and Gillen attended took place after the last ceremony of the black snake, six days after the radius had been brought into the camp.

[239] To simplify the exposition we have omitted a singular rite: the men, decorated with the totemic symbol, stand with spread legs not far from the sacred drawing; the women, in single file, crawl under this sort of arch; the last of them carries behind her back the radius, which is torn from her when she rises to her feet (Spencer & Gillen 1904: 540).

It appears that this rite represents dramatically the same event evoked by the sacred drawing: the ancestor's disappearance underground.

[240] This act is doubtless intended to liberate the soul of the deceased contained in the radius, in the same way as the smashing of the cranium elsewhere (Dubois 1899: 547).

[241] Spencer & Gillen 1904: 740 ff.

[242] Spencer & Gillen 1904: 542, 162.

[243] Spencer & Gillen 1899: 497; but we find in this tribe the exact equivalent of the second obsequies of the northern tribes: this is the ceremony, held twelve to eighteen months after the death, which consists in 'stamping on the twigs of the grave'; its purpose is to 'bury the sorrow' and to inform the soul that the moment has come for it to separate itself finally from the survivors (Spencer & Gillen 1899: 503–9).

[244] During this phase the soul, among the Arunta, bears a special name (ulthana), distinct from that designating the soul of a living person or a disembodied spirit (Spencer & Gillen 1899: 514, 655, 168).

[245] The situation of this place of origin often determines the orientation of the grave or the corpse (Spencer & Gillen 1899: 497; 1904: 508, 542, 554); cf., for the Wotjobaluk, Howitt (1904: 453 ff., 450).

[246] Spencer & Gillen 1904: 277.

[247] Spencer & Gillen 1899: 512, 516, 521; 1904: 450.

[248] Spencer & Gillen 1904: 150 ff., 162, 278, 327; certain ancestors are considered to have been men, others on the contrary distinctly animals, particularly the totem snakes of the northern tribes.

[249] This appears the more astonishing in that among the Warramunga we find the belief that the soul can leave the individual's body even during his lifetime and assume the appearance of his totem: when a man is dead the spirit of his supposed murderer is thought to roam about its victim; to find out which totemic group he belonged to one goes to see if some animal tracks cannot be discovered near the grave (Spencer & Gillen 1904: 526–7).

[250] See Tylor 1903, 2: 236. Cf., on the Zuni, Cushing 1896: 404 ff.— This feature is particularly in evidence among the southern Bantu; cf. Theal (1897: 404 ff.): the souls of members of the clan migrate after death into the body of a sacred eponymous animal.—Similarly in cases of 'individual totemism'; cf., on the Tahitians, Moerenhout (1837, 1: 455–7): the spirit of a deceased person often returned in the body of the very animal that he had revered during his life.

[251] We cite this fact even though there is perhaps no question of characteristic totemism here; we do not know, in fact, if the sacred animal is eponymous or whether it is peculiar to one clan. Note that in the course of the ceremony a person decorated with parakeet feathers represents the soul of the deceased in his present condition (von den Steinen 1894: 504 ff., 511).

[252] We cannot go into an examination here of the rules according to which reincarnation is thought to be effected, and which determine the identity of the individual from the point of view of totemism.

[253] Spencer & Gillen 1904: 34.

[254] Spencer & Gillen 1899: 515; 1904: 546. Perhaps we should relate these facts to what is reported of the Luritcha tribe, which practises cannibalism: care is always taken to destroy the bones of those who have been killed, because otherwise the bones would reunite themselves and the resuscitated victims would exact vengeance from their murderers.

[255] Spencer & Gillen 1899: 507; 1904: 509, 525, 554.

[256] However, among the Warramunga the totemic centres are to some extent concentrated: a limited and particularly rough region would appear to have been the common home of different totemic ancestors (Spencer & Gillen 1904: 250). It is not far from this idea to that of a collective underground stay of the dead: the Arunta believe that ghosts do not like the cold of winter nights, which they pass in subterranean caverns (513).

[257] Perhaps there is more than a vague correlation between these two facts, for one may wonder whether the tree used as the final resting-place for the bones of the deceased, among the Binbinga for example, may not be, or have been, the same as that used as residence by the soul of the deceased; for an analogous fact concerning the depositing of the foreskin after circumcision, cf. Spencer & Gillen (1904: 341) and Frazer (1904: 211). Note that among the Arunta the survival of the souls of the ancestors is linked to the preservation of sacred objects bearing totemic marks, the *churinga*, which they left behind them at the places where they disappeared, to serve as homes for their disembodied spirits (Spencer & Gillen 1899: 123 ff., 132 ff.; 1904: 258, 265–7); now the ritually decorated bones in the more northern tribes seem to be the equivalents of the *churinga*; they form the body of the disembodied spirit; they also are sacred and conceal a magical and fertilising power (531, 546).—In any case, the Warramunga final rite is intended to effect, at least symbolically, the placing of the radius in the local totemic centre.

[258] In studying the totemic final ceremony we have concerned ourselves only with the Australians, but an analogous ceremony must have existed among other totemistic peoples; cf., on the Tlinkit, Krause (1885: 234–8): in a terminal feast in honour of the deceased, the host appears dressed in the insignia of his totem; from without, a member of the family makes the cry of the sacred animal; while the slaves are sacrificed there is a song about the origin of the family and the deeds of the ancestors.

[259] Cf. Riedel 1886: 267; van Balen 1886: 567–8; Müller 1839–44: 63, 72; Rosenberg 1878; 434, 511, 417–19; Turner 1884: 147; Verguet 1885: 208–9; Ellis 1839: 360; Moerenhout 1837: 101–2; Catlin 1842: 89 ff.; Swan 1868: 191–2; Gabb 1875: 497 ff.; Plümacher 1888: 43; Crevaux 1882: 549, 561–2; Batchelor 1877: 30; Grandidier 1886: 225, 227–9. Among the Khevsur all who bear the same family name are united in the same burial place (Radde 1876: 93).

[260] Standing 1883: 73.

[261] Adair 1775: 129 ff., 183.

[262] Cf. in particular Standing 1883: 73; Bosman 1705: 232, 476; Dobrizhoffer 1784: 296–7, 310; Carver 1781: 400–2.

[263] Brinton 1868: 259 ff.

[264] Brinton 1868: 254 ff.; Marcoy, in Preuss (1894: 105) on the Mesaya: they avoid the place in the forest where the bones are put, out of fear that the liberated soul should enter their body.

[265] Von Humboldt 1826, 1: 224–7: some urns appear to contain the bones of entire families.

[266] Squier 1850: 67 ff. 125–30; Thomas 1894: 672 ff., 539; Yarrow 1881: 119, 129, 137, 171; Saville 1899: 350 ff.; Preuss 1894: 10–11, 39 ff.; many hundreds of skeletons have been discovered in these ossuaries. That the bones were placed in these communal resting-places only after desiccation can be demonstrated, at least in a large number of cases: relative position and decoration of the bones, extreme smallness of the coffins (which gave rise to the legend of an extinct pygmy race), etc.; sometimes the bones were heaped pell-mell, sometimes they were gathered together, wrapped and symmetrically laid out.

[267] Yet bodies which had been very recently buried, and which had not yet been attacked by decomposition, were simply cleaned and covered with new clothes; they were buried so at the bottom of the communal grave.

[268] This was followed by a feast, common to the whole village, which was offered by the chief to the dead assembled in the 'big cabin': the central feast seems to have been grafted on to these domestic or local feasts.

[269] The families of the dead mainly met the cost of this liberality. Pieces cut from the clothes with which the bones had been dressed were also distributed: they possessed magical qualities which made them precious.—Brébeuf 1637, 2: 142 ff.; Lafitau 1724, 2: 446–57; Boyle 1889: 5 ff. The account by Brébeuf relates to the Attignauentan, or Bear Nation. For a similar 'feast of souls' among the Iroquois and the Choctaw, see Yarrow (1881: 168–73).—The rite of distributing presents at the funeral feast is particularly stressed among the Northwest Coast Indians and the Eskimo (Krause 1885: 223; Jacobsen 1884: 259; Nelson 1899: 363 ff.; Yarrow 1881: 171 ff.).

[270] Note that the collective character of the final obsequies changes the mode of this reintegration: for the dead of a given period are reunited not with the other dead but with each other. The meaning of the rite is evidently the same.

[271] Precisely at the feast of which we have been given an account, after dissension between two parts of the nation one of them, contrary to custom, abstained from taking part in the ceremony.

[272] Codrington 1891: 261 ff.; this expression comes from the island of Saa.

[273] This danger is sometimes averted by keeping the burial secret (Codrington 1891: 219; Ellis 1839, 1: 405; Moerenhout 1837, 1: 554–5).

[274] Cf. Koch 1900: 34; Gumilla 1758, 1: 316.

K

[275] Man (1882: 86; 1883: 146). There is a characteristic contrast between the sinister abandonment in which the corpse is left during the intermediary period (cf. above, p. 50) and the familiar and kind contact with the bones after the feast.—cf., on the natives of the Sandwich Islands, Campbell (1816: 206–7) and Mariner (1817: Introduction, L); on the Caribs of British Guiana, Schomburgk (1852, 2: 432).

[276] Cf., on the Arawak of southern Orinoco, Raleigh (1722, 2: 201); on the Carib of French Guiana, Biet (1664: 392) and de Neville (1723: 448); on the Jumana and the Tucano, von Martius (1867: 485, 599).

[277] This link is clearly marked in a modern Hindu tale (Monier Williams, in Oldenberg 1903: 476 n. 1): the ghost of a dead person left without burial torments the living until one day a crow drags his bones to the Ganges; he then enters heavenly bliss.—cf. Caland 1896: 107.

[278] *Reports* . . . 5, 1904: 355 ff.

[279] See above, p. 51.

[280] According to Hindu belief the deceased is first a *preta*, a ghost or phantom; he does not enter the world of the *Pitara* until after a certain time (Caland 1888: 22 ff.; Oldenberg 1903: 473 ff.).

[281] See Brinton 1868: 258; Petitot 1886: 37, 150, 461; Brasseur de Bourbourg 1861: 173–7.

[282] Cf. White 1887, 2: 90.

[283] This is the case, for example, among the Abchas: while some of them believe that the soul, delivered by the feast of the fortieth day, goes to rejoin God, others think that it passes into the body of a child born on the same day (Hahn 1900: 244–6).

[284] Petitot 1886: 275 ff.

[285] We know that the name is only one of the elements of the soul.

[286] Nelson 1899: 289, 379, 424 ff., 490; Rink 1877: 206; Cranz 1820, 1: 149, 342; Holm 1888: 111–13, 372–3; Nansen 1894: 228; this giving of the name is obligatory; if it is not given there will be harmful consequences for the child.—Cf., on the Khevsur, Hahn (1900: 212 ff.): when a child one or two years old is ill, the family consults a necromancer in order to find out which soul causes the harm; the sick child is then given the name of the deceased (doubtless with the intention of pacifying the latter by releasing his name-soul and bringing it to life again).—Cf. Petitot 1886: 277; Krause 1885: 282.

[287] Cranz (1820, 1: 149, 342); however, this evidence is contradicted, it appears, by Holm: after the end of the mourning-period the name is no longer pronounced. According to Rink, if the individual dies a short time before the birth, or in particularly painful circumstances, his name cannot be spoken without necessity: the child is given another name for everyday use.—Cf. Jacobsen 1884: 57.

[288] Swan 1868: 189. The duration of the extremely common taboo on the name of the deceased is mostly undefined; yet among the Arunta,

after the ceremony which puts an end to mourning, the name may be freely pronounced except by certain groups of relatives (Spencer & Gillen 1899: 498).

[289] The release of the name-soul is not always accomplished by incarnation in a newly-born child: among several Indian tribes, particularly in the case of a chief or a distinguished person, the name, after being 'locked up with the corpse' for a certain time, is restored by the new chief or some other notable: this is called 'resuscitating the deceased'; the living (chief, etc.) is henceforward regarded as the deceased himself and assumes all his rights. Among the Iroquois this transmigration of the name occasions a great feast, held 'when the sorrows of the family have faded' (Lafitau 1724, 2: 434; Brébeuf 1637: 92); for the Tlinkit, cf. Krause (1885: 234 ff.).—Among the Musquaki Algonkin the person who is charged with taking the soul to the land of the dead, at the final ceremony, adds the name of the deceased to his own: henceforth he represents the deceased and fulfills his familial duties (Owen 1904: 83–6). In this case the 'resurrection of the name' and the introduction of the soul into the land of the dead are closely linked.

[290] Goddard 1903–4: 72. This result is obtained by administering to the relatives of the deceased some magical 'medicine', or by assuring them of the good effects of sacrifice (Junod 1898: 56 ff; Arbousset 1842: 558–65).

[291] Hindu ritual prescribes the erection of a stone which protects the living and serves as a barrier between death and them (Caland 1896: 122).

[292] The Khevsur furnish a typical example of this reintegration (Hahn 1900: 207, 228 ff.): it is effected in the midst of an intense collective joy; there is singing and dancing, and people embrace each other, which at another time would appear scandalous.

[293] See above, p. 58.

[294] Petitot 1886: 119 ff.; Petitot 1886: 271–2.—cf. Alden, in Yarrow 1881: 161 on the Gros Ventre; the corpse is left on the platform where it has been exposed; no one would ever dare to touch it; this would be harmful (bad medicine).

[295] For example, the island Caribs (Rochefort 1658: 568 ff.; Preuss 1894: 19–20).

[296] Cf., on the Pelau Islands, Kubary (1885b: 10): the ceremony is held after 100 days, at the end of the mourning-period; in Java, Crawfurd (1820, 1: 96); on Tonga, Baessler (1895: 335). This recalls the custom still observed by the Jews, not to erect the tombstone until a year after the death.—The ritual closing of the deceased's house among the southern Bantu has the same meaning (Junod 1898: 51, 56; Declé 1898: 233 ff.; cf. du Chaillu 1863: 268 ff.).

[297] One rite is fairly often reported as the essential act in the final ceremony: the destruction, or the burial, or the distribution to strangers, of the clothes or moveable goods of the deceased, which until this are

kept apart; cf., on the Wahpeton Sioux, McChesney in Yarrow (1881: 195); on the Tarahumar, Lumholtz (1902, 1: 384); on the Arawak of British Guiana, Schomburgk (1852: 457–9); on the Khevsur, von Hahn (1900: 230).—The same rite forms an integral part of the ceremony of second burial among various peoples, particularly the Bororo and the Bribri of Costa Rica.

298 Lichtenstein 1811, 1: 423: in the case of a child no more is done than to close the hut in which the death occurred: the contagion does not spread outside it.

299 Man 1883: 146.

300 A passage in the *Vendidad* concerns the definition of the area of contagion of which the corpse is the source; the extent of this area varies according to the higher or lower position assigned to the deceased in the scale of beings. If the deceased is a priest, the defilement spreads over ten people; if he is a warrior, over nine; a farmworker, eight; if it is a herd-dog, seven; and so on. But if the deceased is an idolatrous stranger, or a heretic, or an animal created by Ahriman such as the frog, contact with the corpse entails no defilement of the living whatever; it is during his or its life that such a being was a source of infection; dead, no longer. Even close relatives of the infidel will wear no mourning at his death (Darmesteter 1892, 2: xii ff., 75–8, 105, 190–1, 193, 235, 251).

301 This is clearly expressed in a Maori source: the culture hero Mavi did not wish that men should be destined to die without return, for death seemed to him 'something degrading, and an insult to the dignity of mankind' (White 1887–90, 2: 91).—To diminish the horror of this insult the survivors themselves sometimes wreak a genuine degradation on the deceased. Thus in Tahiti, when the deceased was a member of the Areoi secret society, there was a ceremony held in the temple of this society, and 'the body was stripped of all sacred and mystic power' which the individual was believed to have received from the god at his initiation. Only then could the corpse be buried like that of an ordinary man (Ellis 1839, 1: 244).

302 Or, in Mazdean language, beings of the good creation are only destroyed by the action of the demons, of which Ahriman 'full of death' is the chief (Darmesteter 1892, 2: 68–9).

303 These two causes, moreover, are not mutually exclusive. Cf. Spencer & Gillen 1904: 519; 1899: 48; van Hasselt 1891: 197–8; Forbes 1885: 438; Colenso 1881: 26, 63; Turner 1884, 2: 50 ff., 272; Ellis 1839, 1: 395; Mariner 1817, 1: 374–5; Kubary in Bastian 1888: 5, 47; Dodge 1883: 100; Yarrow 1881: 123; Koch 1900: 38 ff; von den Steinen 1894: 348; Bosman 1705: 224; Kingsley 1897: 459; du Chaillu 1863: 382. These few references, which could be multiplied, suffice to prove the generality of this belief.

304 In China, for example, the death of a father is imputed to his son, who must have lacked filial devotion (de Groot 1892, 1: 69).

305 Godden (1897: 195–6): 'If we could see you we would kill you with our spears! We would eat your flesh! . . . Where have you

fled to? We have no enemy crueler than you, who destroy our friends in our midst.'—Cf. Batchelor 1901: 321, 384–5.

[306] Spencer & Gillen 1904: 516; cf. Kingsley 1897: 463.

[307] See the facts related above, p. 49, concerning the death of chiefs.

[308] This is literally true in societies governed by belief in reincarnation; for then each clan possesses a certain number of souls which it cannot allow to be lost, at the risk of being itself afflicted with extinction.

[309] Recall the passage in the Gospel according to St. John, read in the course of the service for the dead: 'I am the resurrection and the life; he that believeth in me, though he were dead, yet shall he live; and whosoever liveth and believeth in me shall never die.' For him, faith— i.e. the intimate union of the individual to the visible Church—is a token of his future reunion to the invisible Church. This is clearly expressed by the last prayer recited over the grave: *ut, sicut hic eum vera fides junxit fidelium turmis, ita illic eum tua miseratio societ angelicis choris.*

[310] The notion of this resurrection, however, has not changed. Cf. Haigneré (23): 'The body rejoins the soul that has left it; the soul regains, glorious, this body which it leaves for a while to the humiliations of the tomb'; 'the mortal remains of the pious Christian sleep in the grave until the glorious resurrection' (31, 49). Cf. Paul, Corinthians I, 15. 42: the body 'is sown in corruption; it is raised in incorruption'.

[311] We do not say that it always is.

[312] Cf., on the Khevsur, von Hahn (1900: 223): death is 'a passage from impure society to pure and bright habitations'. The soul is pure; the body, the corpse, fetid and impure.

[313] See above, p. 73.—It is remarkable that this representation of death, revealed to us by the study of ethnographic facts, agrees exactly with Christian belief as expounded by a Catholic apologist; cf. Dufour in Haigneré (1888: 60 ff.): 'For the civilised Christian, death, far from being the perpetual exclusion . . . of every person outside the field of universal civilisation, is an initiation into an infinite civilisation and the passage from the earthly to the divine city.' Catholics often have such an intuition of social realities because they share an intense collective life.

[314] See Frazer 1890–1900, 3: 422 ff. Similarly, preparation for sacrifice—i.e. the 'passage from the world of men to the world of gods'— entails the death of the temporal being followed by a rebirth in a new form (Hubert & Mauss 1899: 48 ff.).

[315] e.g. Diels (1890: 48): he explains the parallel between these three groups of rites by the fact that they are all intended to effect a purification. But it is just this, why purification is necessary at these three moments in life, that is to be explained.

[316] Thus birth, like death, must frequently take place outside the house; cf., for example, for the Eskimo, Wells & Kelly (1890: 18); for the Khevsur, Radde (1876: 79, 91).—As in the case of death, the impurity is contagious; it extends to the mother, and often the father, of the newborn child, and imposes on them a life of separation exactly analogous to mourning.

[317] Marriage, like a funeral, implies a grievous parting; the passage from one group to another cannot be made easily; a resistance has to be overcome. We know that a rite of abduction is often an essential moment of the marriage ceremony. Similarly, at a funeral a ritual contest is held between relatives or friends trying to stop the corpse being taken away, and the rest of the community wanting to get the necessary separation over: violence has to be offered to the survivors. Cf., on the islanders of Kar Nicobar, Kloss (1903: 304); for Timor, Gramberg (1872: 212); the island of Roti, Heijmering (1843: 359 ff.); New Britain, Danks (1892: 352); the Pelau Islands, Kubary (1885b: 11); on the Orungu of Cape Lopez, Nassau (1904: 236 ff.).—Similarly the widow is often the object of a struggle between the relatives of the deceased wanting her to rejoin her husband (e.g. on the funeral pyre) and her own relatives who keep her back in the world of the living; cf., on the Tolkotin, Yarrow (1881: 145 ff.).

[318] Cf. Schurtz 1902 and the review of this work in the *Année Sociologique*, VI, 1903: 317–323.

[319] During the wake this flood is generally kept in check, not without suffering, because then we normally have a clear perception—and a lively feeling—of the real: but when thought is relaxed, when the representation of external things is effaced, in the shade of evening or in sleep, the subjective world takes its revenge; then the image, constantly repressed, of the deceased living as before dominates the consciousness. So the state of internal parting and disturbance following a death causes frequent hallucinations and dreams, which in their turn contribute to the prolongation of this state. Cf. Koch (1900: 21).

[320] It is not very important to know whether this new image is destined to persist in the consciousness of the survivors; often the final ceremony abolishes the memory of the deceased; in rejoining the ancestors the deceased is lost in an anonymous collectivity, and he is no longer thought of as an individual. But even forgetting is not a simple and purely negative process: it entails a whole reconstruction.

[321] Cf. Campbell 1721.

[322] The idea of Purgatory is in fact only a transposition into moral language of the idea of a stage preceding final deliverance. The sufferings of the soul during the intermediary period seem at first a consequence of the transitory state in which it finds itself. At a later point in religious evolution the miseries of the soul are conceived as the result and the necessary expiation of the sins it committed during its earthly existence. This transformation, which moreover is quite normal, is exhibited in the Hindu belief concerning the *preta* (Oldenberg 1903: 476 ff.).

[323] It attains this not only by the internal process that we have indicated but often by acts as well. Whatever may be the particular causes determining the institution of blood-vengeance, it is certain that it allows the group to discharge the emotion accumulated in it by the death; this is expressed in the belief that the execution of the supposed

murderer pacifies the soul of the deceased. Thus carrying out a vendetta is often a necessary condition of the final ceremony and of the end of mourning (Steinmetz 1892; Mauss 1897).

[324] It seems likely that the same proposition would be verified concerning changes of state analogous to those occasioned by death. It will be remembered that initiation rites often last a very long time, during which the youth remains in a transitory state which subjects him to numerous taboos. Similarly, the period following marriage (and which in many societies comes to an end only at the birth of the first child) has a special and disquieting character. Finally, physical birth is not enough to introduce a child into the society of the living: the newly-born is the object of representations entirely analogous to those concerning a deceased person. Cf. Cushing 1897: 184; Batchelor 1901: 240.

[325] This is explicitly stated in the Avesta: immediately after the death of a believer the corpse-devil, Druj Nasu, swoops down from the northern regions inhabited by evil spirits 'in the form of a furious fly', and takes possession of the corpse: its presence is marked by the decomposition (Darmesteter 1892, 2: 38 n. 22, 96 ff.).—Analogous representations are current in the Catholic church; cf. Haigneré (1888: 40 ff.): in sprinkling the body with holy water 'the Church seems to intend primarily the putting to flight of the demon whose wild eye glitters with the desire to devour a victim.' Incense is intended to 'overwhelm the infection of the emanations from the corpse, through the pleasing scent of Jesus Christ'.

[326] Among others, Preuss (1894: 239 ff.).

[327] See above, p. 60.—In the interesting little work that we have cited a number of times, Abbé Haigneré clearly stresses the constant parallel between funerary rites and ideas about the soul: 'The Church does with the body what God does with the soul; it follows it from the death-bed to the resting-place . . . it places the body in the bosom of the (consecrated) earth at the moment when it thinks . . . the gate of heaven opens to receive the soul into the bosom of God' (Haigneré 1888: 21 ff., 48–53).

[328] Tromp 1877: 42–4; Grabowsky 1884: 474. It will be remembered that in the same tribe obligatory mourning for an adult lasts 49 days; note that the coffin containing the remains of a child is outside the family sepulture.—Cf., for the Olo Ngaju, Grabowsky (1889: 180): 'the *tivah* is rarely celebrated for children.' The Fjort bury children without delay, the same as poor people and slaves (Dennett 1898: 22).—Similarly, the laws of Manu (Bühler 1886: 180) prescribe that the body of a child not more than two years old shall not be burnt, but shall be buried immediately and the bones never recovered: 'they are left in the forest like a piece of wood, and the impurity of the relatives lasts only three days.' Nevertheless, cremation is optional if the child already has teeth. This last feature recalls the text of Pliny (*Historia Naturalis*, VII: 22): *hominem prius quam genito dente cremari mos gentium non est.*—

Among the Toda both ceremonies, initial and final, are held for children of less than two years, on the same day (Rivers 1906: 391).

[329] Cf. Schwaner 1854, 2: 195; Perham, in Roth 1896, 1: 205; Goudswaard 1863: 70; van Balen 1886: 560–1; von Hasselt 1891: 198; Riedel 1886: 239.

[330] Tromp 1888: 92; cf., on the Tagal of the Philippines, Careri in Blumentritt (1882: 165): 'they imagine that the souls of their ancestors live in the trees.'

[331] Spencer & Gillen (1904: 609): 'the natives believe that the soul of the child returns immediately to its place of origin and may be reborn very soon, very probably in the womb of the same woman.' So infanticide is not a matter of great consequence. Note the contrast with the belief concerning the souls of adults; cf. above, p. 68.—The Algonkin and the Mongols place children less than seven years old by the side of a much-used road, so that their souls may be easily reincarnated (Preuss 1894: 216, 257; cf. Owen 1904: 23).

[332] The Costa Ricans say of a child, not that it has died but that it has rejoined the angels: its funeral is a joyful feast at which tears are banned (Wagner & Scherzer 1856: 196); cf. Lumholtz (1902, 1: 448–9); similarly among the Rumanians (Flachs 1899: 46); among the Bulgarians (Strausz 1898: 452); for Catholic belief, Abbé Désert (1889: 279, 286): *Deus qui omnibus parvulis . . . dum migrant a saeculo . . . vitam illico largiris aeternam.*—The absence, or extreme reduction, of regular mourning for children deceased at less than a certain age is a very general phenomenon: in China, mourning is worn only for children more than eight years old (de Groot 1892–1910: 552, cf. 329, 1075); among the Kayan there is no external mourning for a child which has not yet been given a name (the naming ceremony takes place a month after birth; Nieuwenhuis 1907, 1: 44). Naturally, the individual sorrow of the parents may be very keen; but the social reaction, the obligation to mourn, is lacking.

[333] An analogous explanation accounts for the case when medicine men or ascetics are treated the same as children after death: thus the Sea Dayak hang the bodies of their *manang* in trees (Perham, in Roth 1896, 1: 205); similarly, Hindu ascetics are buried immediately, they 'do not need the sacrament of cremation in order to attain the other world' (Caland 1896: 93–5). By their special practices they are excluded in their lifetime from earthly society; they already belong to the world of the spirits. They are, so to speak, dispensed from death.

[334] Spencer & Gillen 1904: 402 n. 1, 506, 512, 545.—The immediate burial of old persons, contrasting with the normal ritual of double obsequies, is reported also among the Papuans of the Aru Islands (Ribbe 1888: 191 ff.).—The absence (or reduction) of mourning is frequent in the case of aged people: among the southern Sakalav and among the Bechuana it is said of an old person that he has 'gone to sleep', and his obsequies are the occasion of rejoicing (Kurze 1896: 43; Arbousset & Daumas 1842: 475); cf. Gómara 1569: 45 (on the

river-people of Palm River in Florida); Flachs 1899: 62 (on the
Rumanians).

[335] Thus their death is often considered 'natural', not implying
malignant spiritual intervention (von Hasselt 1891: 197–8; Kubary
1888: 3–5; MacDonald 1890: 273; Le Braz 1893, 1: xxii).

[336] Similarly, among the Wollaroi, women are buried immediately
and without great ceremony, which is easily explained since in these
tribes women have no part at all in religious life (Howitt 1904: 467).
Among the Warramunga, on the contrary, the same funeral rites are
held for women and for men; the authors attribute this fact to the belief
existing in this tribe that the soul changes sex at each of its reincarnations
(Spencer & Gillen 1904: 546, 530).

[337] Grabowsky 1889: 181; Roth 1896, 1: 140 ff.; Nieuwenhuis 1907,
1: 91 ff; Forbes 1885: 324; de Clerq 1889: 208; Standing 1883: 73;
Kubary 1886: 78; 1885a: 126. Among the southern Bantu it is forbidden
to weep for a relative struck by lightning, for mourning would be an
act of rebellion against Heaven, which directly caused the death (Arbousset & Daumas 1842: 446; MacDonald 1890: 295; Theal 1897, 7:
401). The corpse of a scalped warrior is merely 'simple carrion' and is
never buried; the soul is thought to be annihilated (Dodge 1883: 101–2,
159).—The prohibition on burying suicides in consecrated ground is
very widespread, as we know, among Christian peoples; cf., for example,
the Irish (Mooney 1888: 287–8) and, on the Bulgarians, Strausz (1898:
454 ff.).—We would draw attention to the characteristic fact that among
the Unmatjera and the Kaitish a young man who has violated tribal
law by marrying a woman who is taboo to him is never exposed on a
platform but is buried immediately (Spencer & Gillen 1904: 512).

[338] Wilken 1885: 197; Chalmers, in Roth 1896, 1: 167; Dodge
1883: 102: the souls of those dead by strangulation remain for ever
near the corpse.

[339] Roth 1896, 1: 219; Kruyt 1895: 29: suicides have a separate
village.—Among the western Eskimo, people who die violent deaths
go to the sky, where they live in sunlight and plenty; the others go to
the subterranean world (Nelson 1899: 423).—Among the ancient
Aztec all men who died in war and all women who died in childbirth
(they are merged with the former) were considered to have been carried
away by the sun and gone to live in the sky: such a death was glorious
and caused only joy to the relatives; drowned persons and those struck
by lightning were the objects of analogous representations (Sahagun
1880: 346, 400 ff., 433 ff.).—We see that we must be on our guard
against identifying people dead in an abnormal way with the damned;
they may equally well be considered as the elect; the two notions coincide
fundamentally in that they both imply a setting apart, a separation.

[340] Remember that souls for whom the *tivah* is not celebrated stay
'dead' for ever.

[341] Junod 1898: 412 ff.: 'The sky, which brings lightning and death,
also presides in a very special way over the birth of twins.'

[342] Cf., for example, Kingsley (1897: 472 ff.); the treatment inflicted on the mother of twins is identical with that to which a widow is subjected: her clothes are torn, her belongings are shattered, she is hunted like an impure thing; she lives like a pariah. A twin who escapes death is a horrifying object whom even his mother would not wish to touch. It is remarkable that in tribes not so far from each other twins are sometimes treated as abominable beings and abandoned to die, sometimes considered as almost divine; but always they are set apart.

[1] Some of which are set out and discussed in Wilson 1891: 149; Jacobs 1892: 22; and Jackson 1905: 41.

[2] See Wilson 1891: 183; Baldwin 1897: 67; and van Biervliet 1899: 276.

[3] Jacobs 1892: 25.

[4] Bastian and Brown-Sequard in Wilson 1891: 193–4.

[5] Rollet 1889: 198; Jackson 1905: 27, 71.

[6] Jacobs 1892: 30, 33.

[7] Wilson 1891: 140, 142.

[8] Wilson 1891: 127–8; Jackson 1905: 52, 97. The latter author estimates those who are naturally right-handed at 17 per cent; but he does not explain how this figure is arrived at. Van Biervliet (1899: 142, 373) does not admit 'the existence of truly ambidextrous persons'; according to him, 98 per cent of people are right-handed. But these reckonings apply only to adults; and he assigns a far too narrow meaning to the word 'ambidexterity'. What matters here is not so much the dimensions of the bones or the strength of the muscles as the possible use of one or the other member.

[9] Jacobs 1892: 33.

[10] Wilson 1891: 139, 148–9, 203. A left-handed person benefits from the inborn dexterity of the left hand and the skill acquired by the right.

[11] See Jackson 1905: 195; Lydon 1900; Buyse 1908: 145. An 'Ambidextral Culture Society' has existed in England for some years.

[12] Cf. (in peasants on Lombardy and Tuscany) Lombroso 1903: 444. Lombroso believes himself to have justified scientifically the old prejudice against left-handed people.

[13] Most of the ethnographic facts on which this study is based come from the Maori, or more exactly from the very primitive Tuhoe tribe, whose conceptions have been recorded with admirable fidelity by Elsdon Best in his articles in the *Transactions of the New Zealand Institute* and the *Journal of the Polynesian Society*.

[14] Our account of religious polarity is only intended to be a rapid sketch. Most of the ideas expressed here will be familiar to the reader who knows the works published by Durkheim, Hubert and Mauss in the *Année Sociologique*. As for certain novel views which this account may obtain, these will be taken up again elsewhere, with the necessary elaboration and proofs.

[15] Some examples of this necessary confusion will be given below. See what is said later about the inferior class of woman, earth, and the left side.

¹⁶ On social dichotomy, see McGee 1900: 845, 863; Durkheim & Mauss 1903: 7.

¹⁷ On this last point, see chiefly Spencer & Gillen 1904: 298.

¹⁸ Note that the two moieties of the tribe are often localised, one occupying the right and the other the left (in camp, during ceremonies, etc.). Cf. Durkheim & Mauss 1903: 52; Spencer & Gillen 1904: 28, 577.

¹⁹ The outline of which exists from a primitive stage: women and children, in relation to men, form an essentially profane class.

²⁰ On the identification of the sky with the sacred element and the earth with the profane or sinister, cf. (for the Maori) Tregear 1904: 408, 466, 486; Best 1905a: 150, 188; 1906: 155. Compare the Greek opposition of celestial to chthonian divinities.

²¹ See especially Best 1905b: 206 and 1901: 73.

²² Best 1906: 26.

²³ See, on the Maori, Colenso 1868: 348, and cf. Durkheim 1898: 40; Crawley 1902.

²⁴ Best 1901: 87; 1906: 161–2; Tregear 1904: 330, 392, 515. Cf. Best 1898a: 241.

²⁵ *Matt.* 6, 3. For the reciprocal interdiction, cf. Burckhardt 1830: 282.

²⁶ McGee has described the dualistic structure of primitive thought from a point of view and in terms rather different from mine. He considers the distinction between right and left as an addition to a primitive system recognising only the opposition between before and behind. This assertion seems arbitrary to me. Cf. McGee 1900: 843.

²⁷ This is the root *deks-* which is met with in different forms from the Indo-Iranian *dákšina* to the Celtic *dess*, passing through Lithuanian, Slavonic, Albanian, Germanic and Greek. Cf. Walde 1905–6 s.v. *dexter*.

²⁸ Concerning these terms (Skr. *savyáh*, Gr. λαιός, Gr. σκαιός, etc.) cf. Schrader 1901 s.v. *Rechts und Links*; Brugmann 1888: 399.*

²⁹ Gr. εὐώνυμος and ἀριστερός, Zend *vairyāstara* (= better), OHG *winistar* (from *wini*, friend), Arabic *aisar* (= happy, cf. Wellhausen 1897, 2: 199), to which should be added, according to Brugmann, the Latin *sinister*. According to Grimm 1818, 2: 681, 689 and more recently Brugmann 1888: 399 the left was originally the favourable side for the Indo-Europeans; these philologists have been deceived by linguistic artifices intended to conceal the true nature of the left. It is certainly a question of antiphrasis.

³⁰ In a letter which he has been so kind as to send me and for which I express my thanks, Meillet had already suggested this explanation (1906: 18).

* [Cf. also C. D. Buck, *A dictionary of selected synonyms in the principle Indo-European languages*, Chicago 1949, pp. 864–5 s.v. 'right', and 865–7 s.v. 'left'. In a comparison of these words from thirty-one languages the author finds that 'there is no such single widespread inherited group for "left" as for "right" '.—R.N.]

[31] Similarly, and for the same reason, 'the names of illnesses and infirmities such as lameness, blindness, and deafness differ from one language to another' (Meillet 1906: 18).

[32] Cf. for example Pictet 1863: 209.

[33] From the low Latin *directum*; cf. Diez 1878, 5: 272 s.v. *ritto*.

[34] Connected with the Skr. *sādhyá*, according to Lidén 1906: 75. Meillet, to whom I owe this note, considers the etymology irreproachable and very probable.

[35] Best 1902: 25; 1904: 236.

[36] Meyer 1873: 26. Cf. Gerhard 1847: 54; Pott 1847: 260. Among the Greeks and Romans the right is frequently invoked in formulas of obsecration; cf. Horace *Ep.* I, 7, 94—*quod te per genium dextramque deosque penates obsecro et obtestor;* see Sittl 1890: 29, n. 5.

[37] Cf. Grimm 1818: 685.

[38] Best 1898a: 123, 133.

[39] Darmesteter 1879, 2: 129 n. 64.

[40] The custom goes back to very ancient times (Egyptian, Greek, Roman). The metal (originally iron, later gold) is endowed with a beneficial virtue which protects from witchcraft: characters engraved on the ring add to its power. The names given to the third finger of the left hand prove its magical character and function: it is the finger 'without a name', 'the doctor', and in Welsh 'the charm finger'. See the articles 'Anulus' and 'Amuletum' in Daremberg & Saglio 1873; Pott 1847: 284, 295; Hofmann 1870: 850. On the word *scaevola* (from *scaevus*, left), meaning a protective charm, see Valeton 1889: 319.

[41] Best 1898a: 130; Tregear 1904: 211.

[42] Or, what amounts to the same thing, the god who sends the message. This explanation, already proposed by the ancients (Plutarch, *Quaestiones Romanae*, 78; Festus 17 s.v. *sinistrae aves*) has been definitely proved by Valeton (1889: 287). The same uncertainties are found among the Arabs: cf. Wellhausen 1897: 202 and Doutté 1909: 359.

[43] The whirling dervishes keep the right hand raised with the palm upwards, to receive blessings from heaven which the left hand, held low towards the earth, transmits to the world below. Simpson 1896: 138. Cf. p. 104.

[44] See Gill 1876: 128, 297. The Hebrew *jamîn*, Skr. *dákshina*, Irish *dess* mean both right and south; see Schrader 1901 s.v. *Himmelsgegenden*. For the Greeks the east is the right of the world and the west the left; cf. Stobaeus, *Eclogae*, I, 15, 6.

[45] This is why the sun is the right eye of Horus and the moon his left. The same in Polynesia (Gill 1876: 153). In Christian representations of the crucifixion the sun shines on the region to the right of the cross, where the new Church triumphs, while the moon illuminates the side of the impenitent thief and the fallen synagogue. See Mâle 1898: 224, 229.

[46] See Simpson 1896; and below p. 104.

[47] Best 1898a: 123; 1902: 25; Tregear 1904: 506.

[48] Eylmann 1909: 376. (I am indebted to M. Mauss for this reference.)

[49] A contemporary physician naïvely formulates the same idea: see Liersch 1893: 46.

[50] The table of contraries which, according to the Pythagoreans, balance each other and constitute the universe comprises finite and infinite, odd and even, right and left, male and female, stable and changing, straight (εὐθύ) and curved, light and shade, good and evil, high and low; see Aristotle, *Metaphysics*, I, 5; and cf. Zeller 1876: 321. The correspondence with the table that I have set out is perfect: the Pythagoreans have simply defined and given shape to extremely ancient popular ideas.

[51] Wilson 1891: 18–19.

[52] Mallery 1881: 364.

[53] Mallery 1881: 414, 416, 420. Cf. Quintilianus, XI, 3. 13 in Sittl 1890: 358 (on the gesture expressing abomination).

[54] See Schrader 1901 s.v. *Gruss*. Cf. Bokhâri 1903: 153.

[55] Bokhâri 1903: 157. Conversely, places haunted by *djinn* are entered left foot first (Lane 1836: 308).

[56] When the left hand intervenes it is only to follow and duplicate the action of the right (White 1887: 197). It is still often ill-regarded (Sittl 1890: 51 n. 2, 88; Simpson 1896: 291).

[57] See Genesis 48, 13.

[58] On *pradakshina* and *deasil*, see Simpson 1896: 75, 90, 183, and especially the monograph by Caland (1898). Traces of this observance are found in the entire Indo-European area.

[59] See Plato, *Laws*, 4, 717a—τοῖς χθονίοις θεοῖς . . . ἀριστερὰ νέμων ὀρθότατα τοῦ τῆς εὐσεβείας σκοποῦ τυγχάνοι; Cf. Sittl 1890: 188.

[60] Gudgeon 1905: 125.

[61] Kruyt 1906: 259, 380 n 1.

[62] Martène 1736, 2: 82; cf. *Middoth* in Simpson 1896: 142.

[63] Simpson 1896; Caland 1898; Jamieson 1808 s.v. *widdersinnis*. Sorceresses present the left to the devil, to do him homage.

[64] Best 1904: 76, 236; 1905: 3; 1901: 98; Goldie 1904: 75.

[65] See *Kauśika sutra* 47, 4 in Caland 1900: 184. Blood extracted from the left side of the body causes death (Best 1897: 41). Contrarily, blood from the right side gives life, regenerates (the wounds of the crucified Christ are always in his right side).

[66] Lartigue 1851: 365.

[67] Lartigue 1851; Burckhardt 1830: 186; Meyer 1873: 26, 28.

[68] This is why beings, real or imaginary, which are believed to possess dreadful magical powers are represented as left-handed: this is the case with the bear among the Kamchadal and the Eskimo (Erman 1873: 36; J. Rae in Wilson 1891: 60).

[69] Usener 1896: 190–1. When the Pythagoreans crossed their legs they took care never to place the left on top of the right. Plutarch, *De vit. pud.* 8. Cf. Bokhâri 1903: 75.

[70] On the Roman *manus*, see Daremberg & Saglio 1873 s.v. *manus*; Sittl 1890: 129, 135. The Romans dedicated the right to good faith; in Arabic the oath is called *jamîn*, the right (Wellhausen 1897: 186).

[71] In Persian, 'give the left' means to betray (Pictet 1877, 3: 227). Cf. Plautus, *Persa*, II, 2, 44—*furtifica laeva*.

[72] See Schrader 1901 s.v. *Gruss;* Caland 1898: 314–15.

[73] Cf. Sittl 1890: 27, 31, 310 (δεξιοῦσθαι, dextrae).

[74] On the importance of right and left in Christian iconography, see Didron 1843: 186 and Mâle 1898: 19.

[75] Cf. (for the Maori) Best 1905a: 199, 221.

[76] Leonard 1906: 310. Neither may a woman touch her husband with the left hand.

[77] On the exclusive use of the left hand for cleansing the apertures of the body 'below the navel', see Lartigue 1851; Roth 1899: 122; Spieth 1906, 1: 235; Jacobs 1892: 21 (on the Malays); *Laws of Manu* V, 132, 136; Bokhâri 1903: 69, 71; Lane 1836: 187.

[78] Best 1902: 25; Tregear 1904: 332.

[79] Tregear 1904.

[80] For example, Carlyle, cited by Wilson (1891: 15); similarly, Cushing 1892: 290.

[81] An account of this is to be found in Jackson 1905: 51, 54. But the weightiest argument has escaped him. It is extremely probable, as has been shown by Deniker (1900: 316) and Schurtz (1900: 352), that the shield derives from a parrying-stick, the manipulation of which required great dexterity. Moreover, there are many peoples who do not know the use of the shield; such indeed are the Maori (Smith 1892: 43; Tregear 1904: 316), among whom the distinction between right and left is particularly pronounced.

[82] Cushing 1892; 1883: 13. Cf. a curious passage on Hermes the Thrice-Great in Stobaeus, *Eclogae* I, 59; and Brinton 1896: 176–7 (on the Chinese).

[83] Just as it may not be touched with the left hand, so the sacred post must not be surprised in its upright state by night or by a (profane) stranger. See Best 1898 b: 627, 656 and Tregear 1904: 225, who follows him.

[84] The thread worn by a Brahman must be plaited from left to right (cf. above, p. 109); plaited the opposite way, it is consecrated to the ancestors and cannot be used by the living (Simpson 1896: 93).

[85] See Meyer 1873: 27; Jacobs 1892: 33.

[86] (1) The system of orientation postulated by the theory, though very general and probably primitive, is far from being universal; cf. Nissen 1907. (2) The heavenly regions are not characterised uniformly: e.g. for the Hindus and the Romans the north is the *regio fausta* and inhabited by the gods, while the south belongs to the dead. (3) If ideas about the sun played the part attributed to them, the right and the left would be inverted among peoples of the southern hemisphere; but the Australian and Maori right coincides with ours.

[87] This constraint is exercised, not only in education properly speaking, but in games, dances, and work, which among primitive peoples have an intensely collective and rhythmic character (Bücher 1897).

[88] It could even be that constraint and social selection should at length have modified the human physical type, if it were proved that the proportion of left-handers is greater among primitives than among civilised peoples; but the evidence on this point is vague and of little weight. Cf. Colenso 1868: 343; Wilson 1891: 66; and, on Stone Age man, Wilson 1891: 31 and Brinton 1896: 175.

[89] In particular, Hamelin 1907: 76.

REFERENCES

L

REFERENCES

BIBLIOGRAPHICAL ABBREVIATIONS USED IN THE REFERENCES

AA   *American Anthropologist.* Menasha.
ARB(A)E   *Annual Report, Bureau of (American) Ethnology.* Washington.
J(R)AI   *Journal of the (Royal) Anthropological Institute.* London.
JPS   *Journal of the Polynesian Society.* Wellington.
TITLV   *Tijdschrift voor Indische Taal-, Land- en Volkenkunde.* Batavia.
TNI   *Tijdschrift voor Nederlandsch-Indië.* Zalt-Bommel-Den Haag.
TPNZI   *Transactions and Proceedings of the New Zealand Institute.* Wellington.

THE COLLECTIVE REPRESENTATION OF DEATH

Adair, James (1775). *History of the American Indians.* London.

Adriani, N. & Kruyt, Alb. C. (1899). 'Van Posso naar Todjo.' *Mededeelingen van wege het Nederlandsche Zendelinggenootschap*, 43: 1–100. Rotterdam.

Arbousset, Thomas (1842). *Relation d'un voyage d'exploration au Nord-Est de la colonie du Cap de Bonne-Espérance.* Paris.

Baarda, M. J. van (1883). 'Ein Totenfest auf Halmaheira.' *Ausland*, 65: 903–5. München.

Baessler, Arthur (1895). *Südsee Bilder.* Berlin.

Balen, J. A. van (1886) 'Iets over het doodenfeest bij de Papoea's aan de Geelvinksbaai. . . .' *TITLV*, 31: 556–93. Batavia.

Batchelor, John (1892). *The Ainu of Japan.* London. (1901). *The Ainu and their folk-lore.* London.

Batchelor, R. T. (1877). 'Notes on the Antankarana and their country.' *Antananarivo Annual* 1, (3): 27–31. Antananarivo, Madagascar.

Baumann, Oscar (1891). *Usambara und seine Nachbargebiete.* Berlin.

Biet, Antoine (1664). *Voyage de la France équinoxiale en l'isle de Cayenne.* Paris.

Blumentritt, Ferdinand (1882). 'Der Ahnencultus und die Religiosen Anschauungen der Malaien des Philippinen-Archipels.' *Mitteilungen der Kaiserlichen und Königlichen Geographischen Gesellschaft in Wien*, 25: 149–80, 197–207.

Boas, F. (1887). 'Notes on the ethnology of British Columbia.' *Proceedings American Philosophical Society*, 24: 422–8. Philadelphia.

Bock, Carl (1881). *The Head-hunters of Borneo.* London.

Bosman, Guillaume [Willem] (1705). *Voyage de Guinée.* Utrecht.

Bovallius, C. (1887). 'Resa i Central Amerika.' Uppsala [review by L. Serrurier in *Internationales Archiv für Ethnographie*, 2, 1889: 76–8].

Boyle, David (1889). 'The Land of Souls.' *Annual Report Canadian Institute:* 4–20. Toronto.

Braches (1882). 'Sandong Raung.' *Jahresberichte der Rheinischen Mission.*

Brasseur de Bourbourg, Etienne-Charles (1861). *Popol-Vuh.* Paris.

Brébeuf, Jean de (1637). *Relation de ce qui s'est passé dans la Nouvelle-France en l'année 1635.* Paris.

Brinton, Daniel Garrison (1868). *Myths of the New World.* New York.

Bühler, G. (trans.) (1886). *The laws of Manu* (Sacred Books of the East, 25). Oxford.

Büttikofer, J. (1888). 'Einiges über die Eingebornen von Liberia.' *Internationales Archiv für Ethnographie,* 1: 33–48, 77–88.

Caland, W. (1888). *Ueber Totenverehrung bei einigen der Indogermanischen Völker.* Amsterdam. (1896). *Die altindischen Todten- und Bestattungsgebräuche.* Amsterdam.

Campbell, Archibald (Hon.) (1721). *The doctrines of a middle state between death and the resurrection.* London.

Campbell, Archibald (1816). *A voyage round the world.* Edinburgh.

Candelier, H. (1893). *Rio-Hacha et les Indiens Goajires.* Paris.

Carver, Jonathan (1781). *Travels through the interior parts of North America* (3rd ed.). London.

Casalis, Eugène (1859). *Les Bassoutos.* Paris.

Catlin, George (1842). *Letters and notes on the manners, customs and condition of the North American Indians.* New York.

Chaillu, Paul Belloni du (1863). *Voyages et aventures dans l'Afrique équatoriale.* Paris.

Chatelin, L.N.R.A. (1880). 'Godsdienst en bijgeloof der Niassers.' *TITLV,* 26: 109–167, 573–579.

Clercq, F. S. A. de (1889). 'Dodadi Mataoe en Gowa ma-taoe of zielenhuisjes in het district Tobelo op Noord-Halmahera.' *Internationales Archiv für Ethnographie,* 2: 204–12.

Codrington, R. H. (1891). *The Melanesians.* Oxford.

Colenso, W. (1881–2). 'On the Maori races of New Zealand.' *TPNZI* 13: 38–57; 14: 3–33.

Cranz, David (1821). *History of Greenland.* (2 vols). London.

Crawfurd, John (1820). *History of the Indian Archipelago.* (3 vols). Edinburgh.

Creagh, C. V. (1897). 'On unusual forms of burial by people of the east coast of Borneo.' *JRAI,* 26: 33–6. London.

Crevaux, Jules (1882). *Voyages dans l'Amérique du Sud.* Nancy.

Cushing, Frank Hamilton (1896). 'Outlines of Zuñi creation myths.' *ARBAE,* 13: 321–447 Washington (1897). 'Remarks on shamanism.' *Proceedings American Philosophical Society,* 36: 183–192.

Cuzent, Gilbert (1872). *Voyage aux îles Gambier.* Paris.

Danks, B. (1892). 'Burial customs of New Britain,' *JRAI,* 21: 348–356.

Darmesteter, James (trans.) (1892–3). *Le Zend-Avesta.* (3 vols). Paris.

Dastre, Albert (1903). *La vie et la mort.* Paris.

Declé, Lionel (1898). *Three years in savage Africa.* London.

Dennett, R. E. (1898). *Notes on the folklore of the Fjort.* London.

Désert, Ch. (1889). *Le livre mortuaire.* Arras.

Diels, Hermann (1890). *Sibyllinische Blätter.* Berlin.

Dieterle, J. Chr. (1883). 'Gebräuche beim Sterben eines Königs in den Tschiländern der Goldküste.' *Ausland,* 56: 754–7.

Dobrizhoffer, Martin (1784). *Historia de Abiponibus.* Vienna.

Dodge, Richard Irving (1883). *Our wild Indians.* Hartford.

Donleben (1848). 'Bijdragen tot de kennis van het eiland Nias.' *TNI,* 10: 171–99.

Dubois, J. A. (1899). *Hindu manners, customs and ceremonies.* Oxford.

Dumont d'Urville, Jules-Sebastian-César (1859). *Histoires générales des voyages.* Paris.

Ellis, William (1839). *Polynesian researches.* London.

Epp, F. (1841). *Schilderungen aus Holländisch Ost-Indiens Archipel.* Heidelberg.

Erman, A. (1870). 'Ethnographische Wahrnehmungen und Erfahrungen an den Küsten des Berings-Meeres.' *Zeitschrift für Ethnologie,* 2: 369–94. Berlin.

Finsch, O. (1885). *Neu-Guinea und seine Bewohner.* Bremen.

Fison, Lorimer (1881). 'Notes on Fijian burial customs.' *JAI,* 10: 137–49.

Flachs, Adolf (1899). *Rumänische Hochzeits und Totengebräuche.* Berlin.

Forbes, Henry O. (1885). *A naturalist's wanderings in the Eastern Archipelago.* London.

Frazer, J. G. (1886). 'On certain burial customs as illustrative of the primitive theory of the soul.' *JAI,* 15: 64–101. (1890). *The golden bough: a study in magic and religion.* London. (1904). 'The origin of circumcision.' *Independent Review,* 4: 204–18. London.

Gabb, Wm. M. (1875). 'On the tribes and languages of Costa Rica.' *Proceedings American Philosophical Society,* 14: 483–602.

Goddard, Pliny Earle (1903–4). 'Life and culture of the Hupa.' *University of California Publications in American Archaeology and Ethnology,* 1: 1–88. Berkeley.

Godden, Gertrude M. (1897). 'Nágá and other frontier tribes of northeast India.' *JAI,* 26: 161–201.

Gómara, Francisco López de (1569). *Histoire générale des Indes Occidentales.* Paris.

Goudswaard, A. (1863). *De Papoea's van de Geelvinksbaai.* Schiedam.

Graafland, N. (1890). 'Die Insel Rote (Rotti).' *Mitteilungen der Geographischen Gesellschaft zu Jena,* 8: 134–168.

Grabowsky, F. (1884). 'Der Distrikt Dusun-Timor in Süd-Ost Borneo und seiner Bewohner.' *Ausland,* 57: 444–9, 469–75. (1888). 'Die "Olon Lowangan" in Südost Borneo.' *Ausland,* 61: 581–4. (1889). 'Der Tod, das Begräbnis, das Tiwah oder Todtenfest bei den Dajaken.' *Internationales Archiv für Ethnographie,* 2: 177–204.

Gramberg, J. S. G. (1872). 'Eene maand in de binnenland van Timor.' *Verhandelingen van het Bataviaasch Genootschap van Kunsten en Wetenschappen,* 36: 161–217. Batavia.

Grandidier, Alfred (1886). 'Des rites funéraires chez les Malagaches.' *Revue d'Ethnographie*, 5: 213-32. Paris.

Groot, Johann Jacob Maria de (1892-1910). *The religious system of China*. (6 vols). Leyden.

Guillain, Charles (1845). *Documents sur l'histoire . . . de Madagascar*. (Annales maritimes et coloniales). Paris.

Gumilla, José (1758). *Histoire naturelle, civile et géographique de l'Orénoque. . . .* Avignon.

Hagen, B. (1883). 'Beiträge zur Kenntnis der Battareligion.' *TITLV*, 28: 498-545.

Hahn, Carl H. von (1900). *Bilder aus dem Kaukasus*. Leipzig.

Haigneré, Daniel (1888). *Des rites funèbres dans la liturgie romaine*. Boulogne-sur-mer.

Hale, Horatio (1846). *United States exploring expedition. . . .* Philadelphia.

Hardeland, A. (1858). *Versuch einer Grammatik der dajakischen Sprache*. Amsterdam. (1859) *Dajacksch-Deutsches Wörterbuch*. Amsterdam.

Hasselt, J. L. van (1891). 'Die Papuastämme an der Geelvinksbaai (Neuguinea).' *Mitteilungen der Geographischen Gesellschaft zu Jena*, 10: 1-14.

Hawkesworth, John (1773). *An account of the voyages undertaken . . . in the southern hemisphere*. London.

Heijmering, G. (1843). 'Zeden en gewoonten op het eiland Rottie.' *TNI*, 6: 81-98, 353-367.

Hendrich, C. Chr. (1888). 'Bootreisen auf dem Katingan in Süd-Borneo.' *Mitteilungen der Geographischen Gesellschaft zu Jena*, 6: 93-110.

Hickson, Sydney J. (1889). *A naturalist in North Celebes*. London.

Hollis, A. C. (1905). *The Masai*. Oxford.

Holm, G. (1888). 'Ethnologisk skizze af Angmagsalikerne.' *Meddelelser om Grønland*, 10: 43-182. Kjøbenhavn.

Howitt, Alfred William (1904). *Native tribes of southeast Australia*. London.

Hubert, H. & Mauss, M. (1899). 'Essai sur la nature et la fonction du sacrifice.' *Année Sociologique*, 2: 29-138. Paris.

Humboldt, Friedrich Wilhelm Heinrich Alexander von (1849). *Ansichten der Natur*. (2 vols). Stuttgart-Tübingen.

Jacobsen, Johann Adrian (1884). *Reise an der nordwestküste Amerikas*. Leipzig.

Junod, Henri A. (1898). *Les Ba-Ronga*. Neufachâtel.

Keating, William H. (1824). *Narrative of an expedition*. Philadelphia.

Kingsley, Mary H. (1897). *Travels in West Africa*. London.

Kleinpaul, R. (1898). *Die Lebendigen und die Toten*. Leipzig.

Kloss, C. Boden (1903). *In the Andamans and the Nicobars*. London.

Koch, Theodor (1900). 'Zum Animismus der südamerikanischen Indianer.' *Internationales Archiv für Ethnographie*, 13—Supplement.

Kolff, Dirk Hendrik (trans. G. W. Earl) (1840). *Voyages of the . . . Dourga*. London.

Krause, Aurel (1885). *Die Tlinkit-Indianer*. Jena.

Krieger, Maximilian (1899). *Neu Guinea*.

Kruyt, A. C. (1895). 'Een en ander aangaande het geestelijk en maatschappelijk leven van den Poso Alfoer.' *Mededeelingen van wege het Nederlandsche Zendeling-genootschap*, 39: 2-36.

Kubary, J. S. (1885a). *Ethnographische Beiträge zur Kenntnis der Karolinischen Inselgruppe und Nachbarschaft*. Berlin. (1885b). 'Die Todtenbestattung auf den Pelauinseln.' *Original-Mittheilungen aus der Ethnologischen Abteilung der Königlichen Museen zu Berlin*, 1: 4-11. Berlin. (1886). 'Die Verbrechung und das Strafverfahren auf den Pelau Inseln.' Orig. Mitt. aus der Ethnol. Abteilung der Königlichen Museen zu Berlin, 1: 77-91. (1888). 'Die Religion der Pelauer.' (*in* A. Bastian, *Allerlei aus Volks- und Menschenkunde*, 1: 1-69. Berlin.)

Kükenthal, Willy (1896-1902). 'Ergebnisse einer zoologischen Forschungsreise in den Molukken und Borneo.' (*Abhandlungen Senkenbergischen Naturforschenden Gesellschaft*, 22-5.) Frankfurt-am-Main.

Kurze, G. (1896). 'Missionar P. Nilsen-Lunds Reise durch das mittlere Sakalavaland.' *Mitteilungen der Geographischen Gesellschaft zu Jena*, 14: 12-47.

Lafitau, Joseph-François (1724). *Moeurs des sauvages amériquains*. (2 vols). Paris.

Lalanne, Ludovic (1847). *Curiosités des traditions, des moeurs at des coutumes*. Paris.

La Neuville, de la (1723). 'Lettre . . . sur l'origine, le pays, et la religion des Guyanois.' *Mémoires pour l'Histoire des Sciences et des Beaux Arts*, 29: 443-55. Trévoux.

Le Braz, Anatole (1893). *La légende de la mort en Basse-Bretagne*. Paris.

Le Gobien, Charles (1700). *Histoire des îles Marianes*. Paris.

Lichtenstein, Heinrich (1811-12). *Reisen im südlichen Afrika*. (2 vols). Berlin.

Lier, van (1901) [notice of communication from]. *Internationales Archiv für Ethnographie*, 14: 216.

Lord, T. (1883). 'The belief of the Sihanaka with regard to the soul.' *Antananarivo Annual*, 2, (7): 93-5.

Low, Hugh (1848). *Sarawak: its inhabitants and productions*. London.

Lumholtz, Carl (1902). *Unknown Mexico*. (2 vols). New York.

MacDonald, James (1890). 'Manners, customs, superstitions and religion of South African tribes,' *JAI*, 19: 264-96.

Maclay, N. von Miklucho (1875). 'Ethnologische Bemerkungen ueber die Papuas der Maclay-Küste in Neu-Guinea.' *Natuurkundig Tijdschrift voor Nederlandsch-Indië*, 36: 66-93.

Man, E. H. (1882). 'On the Andamanese and Nicobarese objects presented to Maj.-Gen. Pitt Rivers.' *JAI*, 11: 268-90. (1883). 'On the aboriginal inhabitants of the Andaman Islands.' *JAI*, 12: 69-175.

Mariner, William (1817). *An account of the natives of the Tonga Islands*. (2 vols). London.

Martius, C. F. P. von (1867). *Beiträge zur Ethnographie und Sprachenkunde Amerika's zumal Brasiliens*. (2 vols). Leipzig.

Maspero, Gaston (1875). *Histoire ancienne des peuples de l'Orient classique*, Paris. (1892–1916). *Etudes de mythologie et d'archaeologie égyptiennes.* (8 vols). Paris.

Matthes, B. F. (1865). *Verslag van een uitstapje naar de Ooster-distrikten van Celebes.* Macassar.

Mauss, Marcel (1897). 'La religion et les origines du droit pénal.' *Revue de l'histoire des religions*, 35: 31–60. Paris.

Meinicke, Carl Eduard (1875–6). *Inseln des Stillen Oceans.* (2 vols). Leipzig.

Meyer, A. B. & Richter, O. (1896). 'Die Bestattungsweisen in der Minahassa.' *Abhandlungen und Berichte des Kon. Zoologischen und Anthropologisch-Ethnographischen Museums zu Dresden*, 9, *Ethnogr. Miscellen*, 1 (6).

Modigliani, Elio (1890). *Un viaggio a Nias.* Milano.

Moerenhout, J. A. (1837). *Voyage aux îles du Grand Océan.* (2 vols). Paris.

Mooney, James (1888). 'The funeral customs of Ireland.' *Proceedings American Philosophical Society*, 25: 243–96. (1894). *Siouan tribes of the East.* Washington.

Müller, Salomon (1839–44). 'Reis in het zuidoostelijk gedeelte van Borneo.' *Verhandelingen van de Natuurlijke Geschiedenis der Nederlandsch overzeesche Bezittingen*, Afdeeling Land- en Volkenkunde: 321–446.

Nansen, Fridtjof (1894). *Eskimo life.* London.

Nassau, Robert Hamill (1904). *Fetichism in West Africa.* London.

Nelson, Edward William (1899). 'Eskimo about Bering Strait.' *ARBAE*, 18: 19–518.

Nieuwenhuis, A. W. (1907). *Quer durch Borneo.* (2 vols). Leiden.

Nuttall, Thomas (1902). *Codex Nuttall.* Cambridge, Mass.

Oldenberg, Hermann (1903). *La religion du Véda.* Paris.

Owen, Mary Alicia (1904). *Folklore of the Musquakie Indians.* London.

Penny, Alfred (1887). *Ten years in Melanesia.* London.

Perelaer, M. T. H. (1870). *Ethnographische beschrijving der Dajaks.* Zaltbommel.

Petitot, Émile (1886). *Traditions indiennes du Canada nord-ouest.* Paris. (1891). *La région du grand lac des Ours.* Paris.

Pinart, Alphonse L. (1873). *Esquimaux et Koloches: idées religieuses et traditions des Kaniagmioutes.* Paris.

Pleyte, C. M. (1885). 'Pratiques et croyances relatives au bucéros dans l'Archipel Indien,' *Revue d'Ethnographie*, 4: 313–18; 5: 464.

Plümacher, O. (1888). 'Etwas über die Goajíra-Indianers.' *Ausland*, 61: 41–60.

Powers, Stephen (1877). 'Tribes of California.' *Contributions to North American Ethnology*, 3. Washington.

Preuss, Konrad Theodor (1894). *Die Begräbnisarten der Amerikaner und Nordostasiaten.* Königsberg.

Rabe, trans. J. Sibree (1877). 'The Sihanaka and their country.' *Antananarivo Annual*, 1 (3): 51–69.

Radde, Gustav Ivanovitch (1876). *Die Chewsur und ihr Land.* Cassel.

'Relation d'une ambassade hollandaise à Bali en 1633.' *Histoire Générale des Voyages,* 17

Reports of the Cambridge Anthropological Expedition to Torres Straits. (6 vols). Cambridge 1901–35.

Ribbe, C. (1892). 'Ein Aufenthalt auf Gros-Seram.' *Festschrift Verein für Erdkunde,* 22. Dresden.

Richardson, J. (1875). 'Remarkable burial customs among the Betsileo.' *Antananarivo Annual,* 1 (1): 70–75.

Riedel, J. G. F. (1886). *De sluik- en kroesharige rassen tusschen Selebes en Papua.* 's-Gravenhage. (1895). 'Alte Gebräuche bei Heirathen, Geburt und Sterbefällen bei dem Toumbuluhstamm in der Minahassa.' *Internationales Archiv für Ethnographie,* 8: 89–109.

Rink, Hinrich Johannes (1877). *Danish Greenland, its people and its products.* London.

Rivers, W. H. R. (1906). *The Todas.* London.

Rochefort, César de (1658). *Histoire naturelle et morale des îles Antilles de l'Amérique.* Rotterdam.

Rohde, Erich (1898). *Psyche* (2nd ed.). Freiburg.

Roos, S. (1872). 'Bijdragen tot de kennis van de taal, land en volk op het eiland Soemba.' *Verhandelingen van het Bataviaasch Genootschap van Kunsten en Wetenschappen,* 36: 1–160.

Rosenberg, C. B. H. von (1878). *Der Malayische Archipel.* Leipzig.

Roth, H. Ling (1896). *The natives of Sarawak.* (2 vols). London. 1903, *Great Benin.* London.

Roth, W. E. (1897). *Ethnological studies among the northwest Queensland aborigines.* London.

Ruete, Said (1899). 'Der Totenkultus der Barabra.' *Globus,* 76: 338–9. Braunschweig.

Sahagun, Bernadino de, trans. D. Jourdanet (1880). *Histoire générale des choses de la Nouvelle-Espagne.* Paris.

Schomburgk, R. (1852). *Reisen der Brüder Schomburgk in Britisch Guiana.* Frankfurt-am-Main.

Schoolcraft, H. R. (1853–6). *Indian Tribes of North America.* (5 vols). Philadelphia.

Schurtz, Heinrich (1902). *Altersklassen und Männerbünde: eine Darstellung der Grundformen der Gesellschaft.* Berlin.

Schwaner, C. A. L. M. (1853–4). *Borneo.* (2 vols). Amsterdam.

Seidel, H. (1896). 'Ethnographisches aus Nordost-Kamerun.' *Globus,* 69: 273–8.

Seler, G. Eduard (1902–15). *Gesammte Abhandlungen zur amerikanischen Sprach- und Alterthumskunde.* (5 vols). Berlin.

Shaw, G. A. (1878). 'The Betsileo: religions and social customs.' *Antananarivo Annual,* 1 (4): 2–11.

Shortland, Edward (1882). *Maori religion and mythology.* London.

Sibree, James (1880). *The Great African Island.* London.

Sievers, W. (1887). *Reise in der Sierra Nevada de Santa Marta.* Leipzig.

Simons, F. A. A. (1885). 'An exploration of the Goajira Peninsula, U.S. of Colombia.' *Proceedings Royal Geographical Society*, n.s. 7: 781–96. London.

Smirnov, Ivan Nikolaevitch, trans. Paul Boyer (1898). 'Les populations finnoises des bassins de la Volga et de la Kama.' *Publications de l'École des Langues Orientales Vivantes*, IVe série, 8. Paris.

Solomon, V. (1902). 'Extracts from diaries kept in Car Nicobar.' *JAI*, 32: 202–38.

Somerville, Boyle T. (1897). 'Ethnographical notes in New Georgia, Solomon Islands.' *JAI*, 26: 357–412.

Spencer, B. & Gillen, F. J. (1899). *Native tribes of central Australia*, London. (1904). *Northern tribes of central Australia.* London.

Squier, Ephraim George (1850). *Aboriginal monuments of the State of New York.* Washington.

Standing, H. F. (1883). 'Malagsy "Fady".' *Antananarivo Annual*, 2, (7): 62–80.

Steinen, Karl von den (1894). *Unter den Naturvölken Zentral-Brasiliens.* Berlin.

Steinmetz, Sebald Rudolf (1892). *Ethnologische Studien zur ersten Entwicklung der Strafe.* Leiden. (1896). *Der Endokannibalismus.* Vienna.

Stevenson, Matilda Coxe (1894). 'The Sia.' *ARBE*, 11: 9–157. (1904). 'The Zuñi Indians.' *ARBAE*, 23: 1–634.

Stevenson, Robert Louis (1900). *In the South Seas.*

Strausz, Adolf (1898). *Die Bulgaren: ethnographische Studien.* Leipzig.

Stuhlmann, Franz (1894). *Mit Emin Pascha ins Herz von Afrika.* Berlin.

Swan, James Gilchrist (1857). *The North-West coast.* New York. (1868). 'The Indians of Cape Flattery.' *Smithsonian Contributions to Knowledge*, 16: 1–106. Washington.

Taylor, Richard (1870). *Te ika a Maori.* London.

Ternaux-Compans, Henri (1840). *Recueil de documents et mémoires originaux sur l'histoire des possessions espagnoles dans l'Amérique.* Paris.

Theal, George McCall (1897–). *Records of the Cape Colony.* London.

Thomas, C. (1894). 'Report on the mound explorations of the Bureau of Ethnology.' *ARBE*, 12: 1–742.

Tregear, Edward (1890). 'The Maoris of New Zealand,' *JAI*, 19: 97–123.

Tromp, S. W. (1877). 'Die Begräbnis bei den Sihongern.' *Berichte der Rheinischen Missions-gesellschaft.* (1888). 'Uit de Salasila van Koetei.' *Bijdragen tot de Taal-, Land- en Volkenkunde van Nederlandsch-Indië*, 37: 1–108.

Turner, George (1884). *Samoa.* London.

Turner, Lucien M. (1894). 'Ethnology of the Ungava district.' *ARBE*, 11: xli–xliii.

Tuuk, H. N. van der (1861). *Bataksch-Nederduitsch Woordenboek.* Amsterdam.

Tylor, E. B. (1876–8). *La civilisation primitive.* (2 vols). Paris. (1903). *Primitive culture.* (4th ed.). London.

Vega, G. de la (1688). *The Royal Commentaries of Peru.* London.

Venjaminov, Ivan, trans. Erman (1849). 'Les îles Aléoutes et leurs habitants.' *Nouvelles Annales des Voyages*, 124: 112–48. Paris.

Verguet, L. (1885). 'Arossi ou San-Christoval et ses habitants.' *Revue d'Ethnographie*, 4: 193–232.

Veth, P. J. (1856). *Borneo's wester-afdeeling*. (2 vols). Zaltbommel.

Voth, H. R. (1905). 'The traditions of the Hopi.' *Field Columbian Museum of Natural History, Anthropological Papers*, 8: 1–319.

Wagner, Moritz & Scherzer, Carl (1856). *Die Republik Costa-Rica*. Leipzig.

Webster, Herbert Caley (1898). *Through New Guinea and the cannibal countries*. . . . London.

Wells, R. & Kelly, J. (1890). 'English-Eskimo and Eskimo-English vocabularies.' *U.S. Bureau of Education Circular of Information*, 2: 1–72. Washington.

White, John (1887–90). *Ancient history of the Maori, his mythology and traditions*. (6 vols). Wellington.

Wilken, G. A. (1884–5). *Het animisme bij de volken van den Indischen Archipel* (2 parts). Amsterdam-Leiden. [Reprinted from: *Indische Gids*, 6, (1): 925–1001; (2): 19–101; 7, (1): 13–59, 191–243.] (1886–7). 'Ueber das Haaropfer und einige andere Trauergebräuche bei den Völkern Indonesiens.' *Revue Coloniale*, 3: 225–79; 4: 345–426. (1889). 'Iets over schedelvereering bij de volken van den Indischen Archipel.' *Bijdragen tot de Taal-, Land- en Volkenkunde van Nederlandsch-Indië*, 38: 89–129.

Wilken, N. P. & Schwarz, J. A. (1867). 'Allerlei over het land en volk van Bolaäng Mongoudou.' *Mededeelingen Nederlandsche Zendeling-genootschap*, 11: 285–400.

Williams, Thomas & Calvert, James (1858). *Fiji and the Fijians, the islands and inhabitants*. (2 vols). London.

Yarrow, H. C. (1881). 'A further contribution to the study of the mortuary customs of the North American Indians.' *ARBE*, 1: 87–203.

THE PRE-EMINENCE OF THE RIGHT HAND

Baldwin, James Mark (1897). *Développement mental dans l'enfant et dans la race*. Paris.

Best, Elsdon (1897). 'Tuhoe Land.' *TPNZI* 30: 33–41. (1898a). 'Omens and superstitious beliefs of the Maoris.' *JPS* 7: 119–36, 233–43. (1898b). 'The art of the Whare Pora.' *TPNZI* 31: 625–58. (1901). 'Maori magic.' *TPNZI* 34: 69–98. (1902). 'Notes on the art of war as conducted by the Maori of New Zealand.' *JPS* 11: 11–41, 47–75, 127–62, 219–46. (1904). 'Notes on the custom of *rahui*.' *JPS* 13: 83–8. (1905a). 'Maori eschatology.' *TPNZI* 38: 148–239. (1905b). 'The lore of the Whare-Kohanga (Part 1).' *JPS* 14: 205–15. (1906). 'The lore of the Whare-Kohanga.' *JPS* 15: 1–26, 147–65, 183–92.

Biervliet, J.-J. van (1899). 'L'homme droit et l'homme gauche.' *Revue Philosophique* 47: 113–43, 276–96, 371–89.

Bokhâri, El (trans. Octave Houdas & W. Marcias) (1903–8). *Les traditions islamiques*. Paris.

Brinton, Daniel G. (1896). 'Lefthandedness in North American aboriginal art.' *AA* 9: 175–81.

Brugmann, Karl (1888). 'Lateinische Etymologien.' *Rheinisches Museum für Philologie* 43: 399–404.

Bücher, Carl (1897). 'Arbeit und Rhythmus.' *Abhandlungen der Königlich Sächsischen Gesellschaft der Wissenschaften* 39, No. 5. Leipzig.

Burckhardt, John Lewis (1830). *Arabic proverbs*. London.

Buyse, Omer (1908). *Méthodes américaines d'éducation générale et technique*. Paris.

Caland, W. (1898). 'Een Indogermaansch lustratie-gebruik.' *Verslagen en Mededeelingen der Koninklijke Akademie van Wetenschappen*, Afd. Letterkunde, 4e reeks, 2: 275–325. Amsterdam. (1900). 'Altindisches Zauberritual.' *Verhandelingen der Koninklijke Akademie van Wetenschappen*, Afd. Letterkunde, nieuwe reeks 3, No. 2. Amsterdam.

Colenso, William (1868). 'On the Maori races of New Zealand.' *TPNZI* 1 [separate pagination].

Crawley, Ernest (1902). *The mystic rose: a study of primitive marriage*. London.

Cushing, Frank Hamilton (1883). 'Zuñi fetishes.' *ARBE* 2: 1–45. (1892). 'Manual concepts: a study of the influence of hand-usage on culture-growth.' *AA* 5: 289–317.

Daremberg, C. V. & Saglio, E. (1873). *Dictionnaire des antiquités grecques et romaines*. Paris.

172

Darmesteter, James (1879). *Zend-Avesta.* London.

Deniker, (J.) (1900). *Races et peuples de la terre.* Paris.

Didron, Alphonse Napoléon (1843) *Iconographie chrétienne: histoire de dieu.* Paris.

Diez, Friedrich Christian (1878). *Etymologisches Wörterbuch der romanischen Sprachen.* Bonn.

Doutté, Edmond (1909). *La société musulmane du Maghrib: magie et religion dans l'Afrique du nord.* Alger.

Durkheim, Émile (1898). 'La prohibition de l'inceste et ses origins.' *Année Sociologique* 1 (1896–7): 1–70. Paris.

Durkheim, E. & Mauss, M. (1903). 'De quelques formes primitives de la classification.' *Année Sociologique* 6 (1901–2): 1–72. Paris.

Erman, (1873). [Comment on Meyer 1873.] *Verhandlungen der Berliner Gesellschaft für Anthropologie, Ethnologie und Urgeschichte* p. 36. Berlin.

Eylmann, Erhard (1909). *Die Eingeborenen der Kolonie Süd-Australiens.* Berlin.

Gerhard, Eduard (1847). *Ueber die Gottheiten der Etrusker.* Berlin.

Gill, William Wyatt (1876). *Myths and songs from the south Pacific.* London.

Goldie, W. H. (1904). 'Maori medical lore.' *TPNZI* 37: 1–120.

Grimm, Jacob Ludwig Carl (1818). *Geschichte der deutschen Sprache.* (2 vols). Leipzig.

Gudgeon, W. E. (1905). 'Maori religion.' *JPS* 14: 107–30.

Hamelin, O. (1907). *Essai sur les éléments principaux de la représentation.* Paris.

Hofmann, F. (1870). 'Ueber den Verlobungs- und den Trauring.' *Sitzungsberichte der Kaiserlichen Akademie der Wissenschaften,* Phil.-Hist. Klasse 65: 825–63. Wien.

Jackson, John (1905). *Ambidexterity: two-handedness and two-brainedness, an argument for natural development and rational education.* London.

Jacobs, Jacob (1892). *Onze rechthandigheid.* Amsterdam.

Jamieson, John (1808). *Etymological dictionary of the Scottish language.* Edinburgh.

Kruyt, Alb. C. (1906). *Het animisme in den Indischen Archipel.* Den Haag.

Lane, Edward William (1836). *Modern Egyptians.* London.

Lartigue (1851). 'Rapport sur les comptoirs de Grand-Bassam et d'Assinie.' *Revue Coloniale,* 2ᵉ série, 7: 329–73.

Leonard, Arthur Glyn (1906). *The lower Niger and its tribes.* London-New York.

Lidén, Evald (1906). 'Armenische Studien.' *Göteborgs Högskolas Arsskrift* 12.

Liersch, L. W. (1893). *Die Linke Hand: eine physiologische und medizinisch-praktische Abhandlung.* Berlin.

Lombroso, C. (1903). 'Lefthandedness.' *North American Review,* 177: 440.

Lydon, F. F. (1900). *Ambidextrous and free-arm blackboard drawing and design.* London.

McGee, W. J. (1900). 'Primitive numbers.' *ARBAE* 19: 821–51.

Mâle, Émile (1898). *L'art religieux du XIIIe siècle en France*. Paris.

Mallery, Garrick (1881). 'Sign-language among the North-American Indians.' *ARBE* 1: 269–552.

Martène, Edmond (1736–7). *De antiques Ecclesiae ritibus*. (3 vols). Antwerp.

Meillet, Paul Jules Antoine (1906). *Quelques hypothèses sur des interdictions de vocabulaire dans les langues indo-européennes*. Chartres.

Meyer, von (1873). 'Ueber den Ursprung von Rechts und Links.' *Verhandlungen der Berliner Gesellschaft für Anthropologie, Ethnologie und Urgeschichte* 5: 25–34.

Nissen, Heinrich (1906–10). *Orientation: Studien zur Geschichte der Religion*. (3 vols). Berlin.

Pictet, Adolphe (1859–63). *Les origines indo-européennes*. (2 vols). Paris.

Pott, Augustus Friedrich (1847). *Die quinare und vegisimale Zählmethode bei Völkern aller Welttheile*. Halle.

Rollet, Etienne (1889). 'La taille des grands singes.' *Revue Scientifique* 44: 196–201.

Roth, H. Ling (ed.) (1899). 'Notes on the Jekris, Sobos and Ijos of the Warri District of the Niger Coast Protectorate.' *JAI* 28: 104–26.

Schrader, Otto (1901). *Reallexicon der indogermanischen Alterstumskunde*. Strassburg.

Schurtz, Heinrich (1900). *Urgeschichte der Kultur*. Leipzig-Wien.

Simpson, William (1896). *The Buddhist praying-wheel*. London-New York.

Sittl, Carl (1890). *Die Gebärden der Griechen und Römer*. Leipzig.

Smith, S. Percy (1892). *Futuna: Horne Island and its people, Western Pacific*. *JPS* 1: 33–52.

Spencer, B. & Gillen, F. J. (1904). *Northern tribes of central Australia*. London.

Spieth, Jakob (1906). *Die Ewe-Stämme*. Berlin.

Tregear, Edward (1904). *The Maori race*. Wanganui, N.Z.

Usener, Hermann (1896). *Götternamen*. Bonn.

Valeton (1889). 'De modis auspicandi Romanorum.' *Mnemosyne* 17: 275–325.

Walde, Alois (1905–6). *Lateinisches Etymologisches Wörterbuch*. Heidelberg.

Wellhausen, Julius (1897). *Reste des arabischen Heidenthums*. Berlin.

White, John (1887–90). *Ancient History of the Maori: his Mythology and Traditions*. (6 vols). Wellington.

Wilson, Daniel (1891). *Lefthandedness*. London.

Zeller, Eduard (1876). *Die Philosophie der Griechen*. Leipzig.